The Breakup Handbook

The Breakup Handbook

How to feel good about a bad breakup

LIANN BROOKES-SMITH

First Edition.

The advice and strategies may not be suitable for every situation. This work is sold with the understanding that neither the author nor the publisher is held responsible for the results accrued from the advice in this book. This book reflects the author's present recollections of experiences over time. These are the author's memories, from their perspective, and they have tried to represent events as faithfully as possible. Names and identifying characteristics have been changed to protect the identity of those in the book and their families.

ISBN 9781739705527 (Hardcopy edition)

ISBN 9781739705503 (Paperback edition)

ISBN 9781739705510 (Ebook edition)

For my wonderful sons, Benjamin and Jacob.

Acknowledgements

This book would not have been possible without those who have supported me on my journey.

My husband Stephen for supporting me to finish this book and accomplish that for myself. To our two little boys, Benjamin and Jacob, I hope this book has set a path for you both to create your own great mindset, finding simple ways to overcome difficult times. You are so loved.

My big brother Bryan and his wife Irena for taking me into their home when I needed it most and always loving me at my worst.

Mum and Dad for telling me I deserved more in life and giving me the skills and determination to always carve out a better path.

My friends who have been on my life journey with me, loving me, sometimes hurting me, being in my sea and my boat in this life. The late nights drinking, partying, dating, being dumped and comparing notes that created the pages of this advice in the first place.

Contents

Preface

I'm a brown-haired girl with a good sense of humour from Birmingham, UK. The kind of girl that would probably be your mate. I'm not the funniest, prettiest or most interesting person in the world, but I am here, and I am consistent. In a TV show, I'd be the character in the background, not grabbing the camera's attention. But for some people, I have become the main character. I am the friend who keeps their phone on at night just in case of an emergency. I am the person who will sit with you for hours and visit you in hospital. Try and think of a unique gift. Am I a good person? To some people, yes. To others, probably not. You can't make everyone happy. I am not perfect; you can only be who you are and do your best. This is who I am.

I have a very expressive face which means I can't lie and get away with it; any genuine thought is right there written across my face. I become emotional at sad films or dramas on the telly. My favourite is a film with a montage, split motivation scenes across dance music leading to fist-pumping glory at the end. I grow mint in my garden because it's pretty impossible to kill. My favourite food is a burrito. My favourite drink is cold tropical juice, and I am partial to an espresso martini.

Yeah, that's me.

Introduction

I've had quite a few breakups over the years. I wasn't the type to settle down long-term with a school sweetheart, so I've had several 'loves' over the years – both long and short-term. What I can honestly say is that none of them played out how you see them in the movies. You know, where the couple falls in love, and the guy fights for the girl through adversity. Meets her at the airport or makes some other dramatic statement. He learns all the little things about her that make her special, tells her how he can't live without her, he understands her habits her mannerisms, her uniqueness, her.

The truth of a real relationship is that you don't see the same story months to years later. You don't see your partner as fun when life becomes routine. When the jerk friend has been offensive. You see the initial dinner dates where you drank, talked and laughed all night, but now you just don't have so much to say anymore. You don't see the times when, after this amazing mixture of events and first holidays that brought you together, suddenly, you don't appear to have plans together, and text messages are no more than a few words.

In my long-term relationships, we've celebrated annual anniversaries. For his birthday, I might have bought hard-to-get tickets for his favourite football team or the champagne spa day, a weekend away with hot tub, a walk behind a waterfall or a trip to Paris. Then all of a sudden, we preferred not being together, the arguments became more serious, more impossible, and we'd start talking about taking a break.

We talked about revitalising the relationship from time to time. Planned special dates. But the nights out we planned reduced down to a night in with a takeaway and bottle of wine, which further reduced to beans on toast and an early night ('early morning start, we don't want a headache') or plans to meet up, which didn't materialize. I've found messages from other girls on their phone making me realize there was nothing to work or fight for. In a long-term relationship, most couples talk every day and see each other regularly if not living together. So when the relationship ends, even though we or specifically I knew it was the right time, it still really hurts.

I've had long-term and short-term relationships that have burned me equally. I'm not a relationship coach or psychologist, but I am aware of patterns, and the information in this book has proved useful to many of my single friends. They have found the advice and fresh perspective helpful and used the strategies to better manage themselves and the situations they find themselves in.

This is the book I wished I had owned at the difficult times. The one that could have helped me deal with my emotions and single life (again). The book that would have consoled me when I was hurting from a breakup. The one that could have reminded me that I wasn't alone in this experience. This book would have changed my day-to-day routine immediately and picked me up every time I read it.

The difference between this book and most other books about breakups, is that I won't be spending lots of time setting out commandments, but I will be giving you handy hacks and tips by which you can implement the ideas quickly and go about your day. There won't be negative language bashing The Ex or wasting time micro analysing them. This handbook will give you lots of solutions to help you move forwards with confidence and positivity towards meeting the love of your life. Throughout this book we will use exercises to deal with what has happened and quickly and positively change your reactions, thoughts and behaviours to move forward as quickly and painlessly as possible.

There is something in here for everyone at every stage of a breakup. I don't believe there are perfect breakups, but there are painful pitfalls to avoid so you can keep unnecessary pain, embarrassment and regret at bay. Wherever you are right now, trust me, you can take your life in both hands every step of the way, like a gazelle leaping delicately across a hazard.

If you were an endurance runner, wouldn't you want to know at which point most people struggle on a route, what they wore and how they prepared themselves for the event? Wouldn't you want a handbook written by an endurance runner to know how they did it? How do they make themselves run when they don't feel like it, how do they overcome the negative self-talk? You'd want to know how to overcome all the challenges mentally and physically.

In *The Breakup Handbook*, you'll discover strategies to keep you motivated to be your best self, help you experience more self-love and feel excited about the life you have ahead of you.

When you are in a relationship you become a person that fits into that relationship. When I was single, I was reeling with unanswered questions. *Who was I in the relationship? Who am I now? What has life got in store for me in the future now I'm single? What do I want from life going forward, and what's the plan now?*

In the following weeks, I noticed when I felt energized or so low that I didn't want to get out of bed. I observed new patterns in my behaviours – whether they were hindering me or helping me. I also noticed those around me and how their behaviour boosted or sabotaged my progress. It was like I was standing back, watching my interactions, and I could see where I was going right or wrong. I started to catalogue some personal guidelines to help me feel better, traps I needed to avoid, perfect solutions and positive activities to help me overcome that feeling of being kicked in the stomach. I decided to write *The Breakup Handbook.*

The good news?

I came out the other side the best me, and now I want to share what I learned with you. Some of these hints and tips are useful for other areas of life, not just breakups, and have proved valuable in dealing with friends and even at work. You'll also find hints and short exercises/ideas throughout the following chapters, so you might find it helpful to keep a notepad and pen handy as you read.

Feeling lost and what to do next

You likely picked up this book because you've split up from a significant other and need help on what to do next. You want to avoid the whole embarrassing heap of a mess that can happen after a breakup and come out the other side stronger, better and happier. I'll be with you every step of the way, cheering you on and helping you create those positive actions and thoughts that will help you move on quicker, easier and hopefully with a lot less pain.

They say breakups are never easy, but there is no reason why you can't recognize a relationship has ended for a good reason, even though it hurts to lose someone you've loved and cared for. By reviewing your routines, trends, mindset and thought processes in the following chapters, you'll learn how to identify and address the source of the pain to move through it and onwards into a brighter future.

You might experience flashbacks: how you got together, the times you let unfair things slide to the forefront, those times you had it really good, when you were unnecessarily difficult, when they let you down, and how you put yourself out there for them. But you can turn those heart-breaking and heart-sinking moments into more positive, calmer and motivating situations.

From this book you will gain perspective on why you feel like you do and how you can use that knowledge to dodge obstacles in your way. In fact, before long, you'll see how your breakup is a good thing.

I wanted to find ways to come out of my breakup on top – living life to the full and rocking it. What I didn't realize was that there are so many other factors that impact recovery. Your environment and the people you have around you is a massive part. I found perfect solutions to all the pitfalls so you can use them to your advantage.

I'm sure you'll find the events described here reflect your experiences at some point, and the advice helps you find the strategy you need to overcome whatever you're facing. You won't find much of what I am sharing in your typical relationship guide, as I'll work through the various experiences and scenarios with solutions to counteract them. It's good to have plans to move through any challenging feelings and divert them when they arise.

The opposite of loving someone is not hating them.
It's not thinking of them at all.

Chapter 1

The Aftermath of The Ex

Let's start by looking at the events and experiences in the initial breakup phase. You may have experienced some of these events already and will read through the following list thinking, *yes, that's 100 per cent me,* or you may have picked this book up early and haven't experienced them yet. Keep reading so you're fully aware of what can crop up for you. Also, it's good to recognize that your experiences and even your thoughts are very common and happen to most people.

The reasons relationships end are different and complex; each has its own set of circumstances. No two people are the same, and no two couples are the same, yet there are similarities. We go through similar processes to heal and move on. We all want to come out the other side stronger and with a reduced likelihood of it happening again.

These issues can crop up for you, whether it has been a short- or long-term relationship. I have found the sudden split in a short-term relationship after intense feelings of connection can hurt more than a longer-term relationship that has burnt out some time ago.

Understanding why you're thinking of The Ex

Whether you're the one who made the break or not, you'll probably notice that you will be thinking about The Ex – a lot. This stage can feel quite overwhelming. If your partner had passed away, family and friends would expect you to mourn for a period of time, however because they are still very much alive, that social permission is not there to take time to come to terms with what has happened. It is often felt that you need to just get on with things from day one.

Much of what you will read in this book are definite solutions that have been proven to help people move on quicker, but let's not forget that it is also OK just to feel more than a little sad about what has just happened. I just do not want it to be a defining feature of your day and definitely not last long.

So many times, I have heard people say that it takes the same amount of time to get over someone as you were together or something to that effect. They have described in great detail that you must go through the stages of mourning before you can move on. I believe, yes, there are stages, however, when moving on from a breakup myself and then watching my friends do it too, I could see that whatever you think *should* happen, *will* happen. If you think it should take 5 years to recover from a breakup, then somewhere in your mind, you make a decision that this is true and that becomes your reality. If you state that you will mourn The Ex, then that is what you will do. My ask from the reader, is to decide what you want your future to be.

I've asked people what they would rather do:

1. fully understand why things did not work with The Ex and get closure, or
2. meet the love of their life in two years.

I have found that everyone has always stated the second, they would rather meet the love of their life. Yet, until I asked this question many were dead set that they needed closure from The Ex, that they wanted to understand what happened; and because of this mindset they would allow thoughts of The Ex to bring them down. They would have their day turned upside down or turn down plans at the final moment because of The Ex posting on social media. This inner turmoil prevented them from getting out in the world and meeting the love of their life.

Yet knowing a new partner was a certainty changed all other thoughts and allowed them to switch off and focus on the future, without a second thought for The Ex. These types of exercises are useful to bump you out of a lull and into moving forward.

The more you believe you should be struggling with the breakup, the longer you will.

I was even able to get control of the physiological elements of the breakups that I didn't think I could change immediately, such as waking up at 3am, losing hair, getting frequent colds and that stomach sinking feeling when I first awoke. The more I stopped the negative and sad thinking from dictating the rest of my thoughts, the easier those days were and the more happier I became.

These processes of the brain can be hacked so although you have broken up from a meaningful relationship, you short cut around these thoughts to get to the brain pathways that lead you to feeling happier and remaining happier.

Whether you have been with them for three months or 30 years, there are many reasons why you can't get The Ex out of your head. You will think of them because you loved them and you miss them, but the brain's interpretation of 'missing them' is actually a mix of biology (brain chemistry), ego[1,2] (the 'self' interacting with the outer world'), thought processing (interpretation of the full picture of the relationship) and habit (routines).

- You loved them: biology and brain chemistry. There was a chemical attraction – similar to addiction, not receiving it creates depressed mood and even withdrawal.
- The feeling of rejection sparks feelings even if you no longer want to be in the relationship. You are hurt by what has happened – this is the ego (the impact on the self).
- You feel you have areas you want to get more information on, events that happened in the relationship where you feel you do not have the full story. A feeling you want the truth, closure and/or to have your say.
- You had memories of great times together, they were part of your daily or weekly routine. You had anchored thoughts of them to key points in your daily habits.

1. Chemical attraction

There has been a massive amount of scientific research into attraction[3,4,5] and its impact on the brain. It has been scientifically proven that when

1 Claude, S. *Scripts People Live: Transactional Analysis of Life Scripts.*
2 Berne, E. *Games People Play: The Psychology of Human Relationships.*
3 Wu, K. `Love. Actually: The Science Behind Lust, Attraction, and Companionship', 14 February 2017. Accessed 14 February 2022: https://sitn.hms.harvard.edu/flash/2017/love-actually-science-behind-lust-attraction-companionship
4 Esch, T. & Stefano, B. 'The Neurobiology of Love'. Neuroendocrinology Letters, ; 26(3):175-92. Accessed 14 February 2022: https://www.researchgate.net/publication/7752806_The_Neurobiology_of_Love
5 Aleksidze, N. 'The Quantitative Distribution of the Hormones of Love and Neurotransmitters at Psycho Emotional Stresses'. Journal of Neurology, Psychiatry and Brain Research, 2019. Accessed 14 February 2022: https://www.researchgate.net/publication/327422320_The_Quantitative_Distribution_of_the_Hormones_of_Love_and_Neurotransmitters_at_Psycho_Emotional_Stresses

you're first attracted to someone, the brain releases a cocktail of chemicals/ hormones. These chemicals are released whenever you interact with this person – from hearing their voice or feeling their passing touch to eye contact. This particular cocktail includes some of the most addictive and stimulating of the brain's chemicals. These are:

- **Oxytocin:** The love chemical – generates feelings of love and wellbeing. Oxytocin is released at birth in huge amounts and underpins unconditional love and elation.

- **Dopamine:** The pleasure/reward chemical – creates feelings that tell the body it wants to 'do it again.' Dopamine creates reward-seeking loops in the brain. Other dopamine stimulants include foods like chocolate, exercise, nicotine and recreational drugs such as amphetamines and heroin.

- **Serotonin:** The happiness chemical – a mood stabilizer that generates pleasurable feelings.

- **Endorphins**: Pleasure chemicals – that create the feeling of euphoria; they also reduce pain and discomfort.

The most addictive recreational and pharmaceutical drugs increase dopamine levels. When the brain attaches those feelings to another person, it makes sense that you want to see them again, hear from them, touch them. So breaking up with someone is on par with removing yourself from a drug. First of all, feeling the downs following a high, then the withdrawal feeling of wanting that hit of good feelings again.

You may feel scatty and jittery because you need that chemical hit. Your brain knows that you will get that when you see and hear from The Ex. Your brain is telling your entire nervous system, 'I want that again...

and again… and again.' So when you're no longer able to see or hear from that person, your body screams at you to find a way.

At the beginning of a relationship, you'll notice that when you receive a text or see your partner, you may feel massive relief, but after a while, this feeling wears off, and you want to hear from them again. You may question whether they like you, in the same way that someone addicted to substances may worry they don't have any more supply. You can't control who gives you this chemical release, and sometimes it can be someone you don't necessarily want to have a relationship with.

You are literally addicted to this person at this current time; like any drug, you need to wean off this. Just being aware that this isn't you, these aren't your thoughts, this is your physiology craving the effect this person has on you. When you have been in a longer-term relationship, these initial feelings can dampen down, but return during the breakup.

The chemical description of a 'crush' is meeting someone who causes your brain to release the four attraction chemicals: oxytocin, dopamine, serotonin and endorphins.

Sometimes the other person can say or do something that tells your brain, 'This person no longer stimulates these chemicals for me.' You just don't get the release of attraction chemicals anymore. You may not be conscious of this, but you just can't put your finger on why it is you stopped liking them.

I have been liked by someone who told me that they thought about me all the time and couldn't wait to see me, but I just wasn't attracted to them in the same way. I have also liked someone so much my tummy knotted at the thought of bumping into them. When they have spoken to me, I have felt my cheeks burn bright red. But it was clear from their passive actions towards me that they didn't like me in the same way.

2. Rejection is never good

No one likes to be turned down or told they aren't good enough, be it a job application, a friendship or a relationship. I was talking to a guy in a club once, with no intention in it whatsoever, I was just making small chat in a queue for the bar. Out of nowhere he pointed out that I was very nice, but he didn't want a relationship with me. This may have been game play or him just wanting to be clear, even though dating him was the last thing on my mind. Equally I was not attracted to him in the slightest. However, him pointing out that he was not interested in me, even though I was not in any way attracted to him, hurt. It bizarrely hurt. Even though I would wholeheartedly agree that I didn't want to date him, I felt rejected from something I didn't even want!

Being told by someone you like, that they don't want to be with you or that they don't feel the same way hurts. It raises questions in your mind: *Am I good enough? What am I missing? What does she have that I don't? No one will ever like me. There must be something wrong with me. Why am I not enough?* This can consume you, making you feel you need to change who you are and what you're about.

The difficulty with relationships is you either click with someone, or you don't. If they don't feel the same way, it doesn't mean anything is wrong with you. You don't need the right qualification, makeup or walking shoes to fall in love. The brain does what the brain does. When you meet someone, it can spark something, or it's a damp squib. Sometimes you can be with someone, and the feeling fades even when you don't want it to. Sometimes you've known someone for years before you suddenly start to have romantic feelings for them.

I had logged all the things I wanted in my perfect partner in my mind, all the things that I thought I wanted in a boyfriend. But, I have fallen for someone who didn't quite fit it all and felt nothing for guys who were perfect matches for what I thought I wanted. The bottom line is no one can pretend their way into someone's heart, and neither should you want to. Who wants to spend life being someone they're not? You need a partner that will love you for you. If you didn't create that spark for them, you can't feel rejected or rather, you should try not to feel rejected because they cannot help how they feel. It's not something you or they can create. You either have what their brain connects to, or you don't.

The most beautiful women and men in the world also have their fair share of times of not creating a spark for someone. No one is immune to being rejected by someone they like.

When you meet someone that loves you for you, that's not fate. There are millions of people out there that would light the spark and be a good partner for you. The kind of people who don't require you to pretend to be something you're not, because they are into all the things that make you, you. You are also into all the things that make them, them.

I once dated a guy who seemed perfect. He was such fun, great company and we laughed a lot together. We would send each other funny gifs, we both wanted to explore and see the same things. We would have great times out together and had a lot in common. However, he didn't create this feeling of love, excitement or passion. It was like being with my friends or family. I think I hoped because he was so funny and good to be around that it would come. But it didn't. So it ended.

If I felt that this guy would try to change himself to make me fall for him, I would have been gutted. He was wonderful, caring, funny, good looking, smart, stylish and successful. There is nothing that he needed to do to be everything I ever wanted in a guy. But the feeling just didn't come. I just didn't feel that crush, that spark, no matter how much I tried. I told myself to relax, and it would come, but it didn't. I genuinely think that the girl he eventually married got the most amazing guy. I wish I could have felt the right feelings for it to have been me.

I use that example whenever it doesn't work out with someone I am dating, or they ghost me. I remind myself that this isn't rejection, they *just aren't feeling a connection for me, and that's OK.* They can't help it in the same way that I couldn't.

3. Unresolved discussions and arguments

Not everything can be said in any one moment, so you have all these things you haven't said stored up, or as time progresses on from an argument, you come up with a response you wish you had said instead.

Perhaps you go over old issues and argue it out in your head. Even if you're desperate to have a row with them over the phone, text or email, The Ex is no longer available or present to discuss these with you every minute of every day. If you cannot have these fights with the person themselves and you have so much more you want to say, then in your head is where they will have to happen.

Not every feeling can be felt in the moment. At the time, you may have felt numb or didn't care, but now you're angry and have a different point of view. What was said when you talked may not have sunk in at the time; now you see another side, another viewpoint. New information may have come to light, or other parties may be involved. You may feel wronged, and they equally may feel wronged by you and pushed you away. Or you have been wronged, and they really don't care about that. You could even question whether a boundary has been breached or whether you should have compromised.

Not only are we taking in information moment by moment, but we also need processing time to understand it. Flipping it back and forth, adding it to other information and creating a context. On its own, updated information may be quite innocent, but when you add it all together, you realize it's not quite as it seemed. For example, your partner may imply they think it's time you split, they have become bored in the relationship, that you are the reason why you both don't do things together anymore, or the spark has fizzled out. When in fact, you've tried to book things and suggest things to revitalize things, but they have worked late or weren't in the right frame of mind. As such you feel that you had worked to keep it together, and your partner's statements were unfair or incorrect.

You may have seen that the relationship had issues and accepted them as par for the course for a long-term relationship. Now, the knowledge that the issues are big enough to split up can be a shock. As can realising you can't be with that person anymore. It can make you question whether you're acting irrationally and making the right decision. This processing, adding stuff together and contextualising is part of your brain coming to terms with what has just happened. It's necessary to do this, so you'll be thinking of them, no matter how much you try not to.

4. Your daily routine, anchors and reminders

Over time we develop routines of interacting with our partners. These little rituals can take many forms, so when our other half becomes The Ex, those familiar routines are lost too. For example, you may have had the same joke every morning about the toothpaste, how they had to use a specific cup for their coffee, or how they squeezed their teabag or ordered the same meal. You have in-jokes and shared opinions. And then there's the favourite seat in the house or coffee shop that you still walk past. There may be a monthly or yearly event that you always went to together without fail.

Not only are your daily routines missing The Ex, but because they have been part of that, these things become anchors to memories and thoughts of them. When we split up, that energy, the sharing of those thoughts, that process has nowhere to go, which disrupts our usual routines and makes us . . . you've guessed it, think about them.

How your mind fills the gap

In place of messaging The Ex and sharing news or conversation, get ready to think about them and even talk to them in your head. Although you may no longer see The Ex, there may be plenty you wish to say to them, including things that have occurred since the breakup.

In the absence of The Ex in my life and the familiar process of thinking about him, my brain was at a loss. I'm not suggesting I was obsessive, but The Ex was a fundamental part of my day and week, if not the centrepiece from time to time, and then he definitely became the curtain and chairs in the room of my life.

I wouldn't make plans without checking with him first, as The Ex always remembered if we had tickets for something or had agreed to meet others. If he was out for the night, I might make plans because I didn't always like being home on my own. Sometimes I relished the solitude. I would paint my toenails and listen to an audiobook with a glass of wine, secure in the knowledge that he wasn't in earshot. It's not that I couldn't do these things when he was home; they were just activities I did when he wasn't. That's how I lived around The Ex.

When the relationship ended, there was nothing. It was like sitting in a living room without chairs and curtains and not being allowed to miss the chairs or curtains or talk about them.

After our breakup, when I was working at my desk, I would tell myself to stop thinking of him and get very frustrated. My brain was confused or in shock. What was it to do now? My brain was in the habit of talking to this person every day. I was used to wondering how his day went. Whether that boss got that promotion etc. In his absence, I tried to generate unique information about him – a new viewpoint. It's like my brain wanted to fill the void of him not being present by finding alternative information. This manifested itself in several ways:

1. Talking to him in my head because we shared things with each other all the time until the split.
2. Re-evaluating information and trying to see different angles on the same course of events, messages, emails, photos of us together.
3. Other people's viewpoints on the same course of events.
4. Trying to get information on his life after the split – e.g. by scouring social media.

1. Silent conversations

Throughout the day, I had imaginary conversations with The Ex. In these mental discussions, I covered every conversation eventuality. We had conversations whereby he was sorry and desperately wanted me back.

In return, I would tell him what he needed to say for me to forgive him. He would say he had obviously made a mistake losing me and would do anything to make things work. There were conversations where I begged him to come back, trying to explain to him why we were right for each other, but he wouldn't hear it. There were conversations whereby we would discuss how to avoid this happening again. I even had dreams in which he didn't want to know me, or he sent me a letter apologizing and, worst of all, dreams where we were still together.

I'd talk with him in my head about where we got it wrong or where we could have been better as partners. Sometimes I expressed bitterness for giving everything to this unthankful selfish person or went over when we'd been there for each other or let each other down. Everything was up for discussion in my head.

2. Re-evaluating the relationship

Sometimes I read old email chains, old text messages from earlier in our relationship and more recent ones to view the contrast. I looked at old photos from holidays, nights out with friends or just with each other – to see what I had missed. I constantly re-ran various interactions in my mind. I think my brain was attempting to find a cure for the situation or understand where our relationship had started going irreversibly downhill, perhaps in the hope of finding an answer. Maybe to understand it enough so I wouldn't get hurt again. Perhaps I could fix things. Did I want to fix things? Is this for the best? Was I happier now it was over? In some scenarios, this was the best thing for me, and I was happy the relationship had ended. In others, I was a victim of his decisions. I analysed and reassessed nonstop, it was exhausting.

3. Different perspectives

I often moved on to having conversations with friends and collecting their viewpoints on the breakup, reviewing old messages in this new light of their interpretation of our relationship from the interactions they'd observed. Whether we seemed like a good fit in the first place. What I should do now and next. I didn't always need to bring this up, as friends often asked about it. I guess it was semi-interesting and gave them something to talk about. The new viewpoints sometimes surprised me, crawled under my skin and kept me up all night.

I remember one specifically. I met with a friend quite soon after the breakup. She said The Ex wasn't right for me, and things had been off for a while. She said something along the lines of: 'Remember that party last September for our friend? He seemed to speak to that one girl quite a lot and didn't seem to want to talk to anyone else. I tried to talk to him, but he seemed really off and stonewalled the conversation to keep talking to that girl. I tried to talk to you about it at the time, but I didn't want to upset you.'

I had to pull the memory of the party out of my mental archives. I remembered The Ex hadn't wanted to go to the party, and we'd had a row in the taxi home because he said I left him mostly on his own and had no one to talk to. He had met my friend a few times, so he did at least have one other person to talk to. I had noticed him talking to the girl for a long time but had been busy setting up stuff and getting the cake and was appreciative that he'd found someone to talk to.

As my friend continued talking about her work and updating me on her dad's trip to the hospital, I was only half-listening – too busy cataloguing and contextualising this story about The Ex. The party was nine months ago, shortly after he and I were having more discussions about making things work. I had thought he was just talking to a girl and really didn't want to be at the party but now wondered if he'd been flirting. Maybe he was playing games, thinking I'd get jealous and want to leave the party; but it didn't work. Maybe that is why he was angry in the taxi. Maybe him being angry in the taxi was a way of deflecting from his obvious flirting? I knew I couldn't ask him about it, so it was more evidence that we should have broken up earlier. But this small conversation with my friend upset me, and I went home earlier than I'd planned and went straight to bed.

4. Acquiring new information via social media

Worst of all was my brain attempting to create a context for what I saw on social media. I would remind myself that we had broken up, and it was up to him what he posted. But I was always disappointed if there was something new on his page as I didn't want to see new post-us pictures. But I was also disappointed when there wasn't anything new to see. I would even check out his friends' posts to see if I could spot him. From time to time, there were new photos of him on a night out. I would first look at all the pictures with him in, then try and work out if there was anyone out with him that night he was trying to be with. I would look in the background of photos to see if I could spot him talking to anyone. All the while trying not to accidentally "like" anything or leave a digital footprint.

How to stop being stuck on repeat

So I was stuck on repeat, thinking of him, telling myself not to think of him, acquiring more information and feeling low. Wondering: *Is he moving on? Is he missing me? Is he also overthinking why we split up? Is he happy? Has he met someone else? Had this breakup been coming for a long time?* The more I wanted to stop thinking of The Ex, the more the thoughts of him dug their heels in.

I understood he was a habit. After spending so much time with someone, it feels odd to no longer be on speaking terms. My friends and family said it was 'weird and needy' that I wanted to speak to him. But the Ex was a big part of my headspace. We'd talked about marriage and growing old together, and my heart and head couldn't just forget that. I wanted to speak to him about the breakup, to tell my old best friend that I was hurting, but I couldn't because he was the source of my pain.

Overthinking a breakup is natural but these thinking processes can be hacked to stop negative thinking and move to more positive future thoughts.

This pattern needs to be disrupted. As we will cover later on in this book, the four types of thoughts I've described here can be overcome. Know that your chemical addiction to them reduces the longer the time goes that you aren't in touch with them. The more time that passes between your interacting with The Ex and not creating new information on them, the better. The main action is to stop the four ways in which your mind tries to acquire new information on The Ex. Your mind is in a pattern of thinking about them, which needs to be broken.

We will look at building confidence to reduce the hurt that comes with feeling rejection, so you can feel your best, and be a better and more confident version of you.

Cyclical arguments and discussions in your head can be very distracting. Later on in this book we look at how to create closure on those arguments, so that they don't keep going around in your head.

Finally, routines, your environment and other triggers reduce how much you are prompted to think of the Ex. I will provide strategies to prevent this and move on quickly.

In a nutshell

- Breakups are difficult regardless of whether your relationship was short- or long-term, the feelings can be just as intense.
- We often hear that breakups can take a while to recover from. If you decide that your breakup will be hard, it will. If you decide you will move on quickly and painlessly, that will be your reality.
- We find we are overwhelmed by thinking of The Ex. This happens for many reasons, which come under the areas of biology (attraction hormones, how we feel), ego (the shock and hurt of rejection), processing information on what has happened (unfinished arguments) and routine and habits (part of your life, memories together).
- To help you to move on, accept that your mind has a gap to fill, and it may find many ways to fill it: talking to The Ex in your imagination, going over old events in the past, speaking to others about The Ex and looking for new information about The Ex, i.e. their social media feeds.
- Know that all of these thoughts and feelings will pass in time. Accepting these as normal and not beating yourself is the best way to be kind to yourself. As we move through this book, we'll look at tactics to overcome or reframe these difficult thoughts and move on more easily.

Get out your notebook

- Write down the things you're mostly thinking about when it comes to The Ex.
- Really dig into the origins of these thoughts now that they are out of your head. After each one write which category it is, such as: "feeling/love/attraction," "feeling hurt/rejected," "unsettled arguments" or" routines."
- When do you find yourself thinking each thought the most? This can include times or places such as days of the week or passing certain venues or even in situations such as when you are most tired, when you stay up late alone.
- Look though the list of ways in which your mind tries to generate new information on The Ex. Are you finding that you are doing these frequently, are there immediate actions you can take now to reduce information on The Ex?
- Once you have the list and identify which categories they fall under, call these thoughts out. Say to yourself, "this is just my brain wanting some good feeling hormones!" "This is just my brain wanting to rerun events to gather more information". "This is because I walked past that cafe". That is all this is. "It doesn't mean anything it's just your brain being prompted by your environment".
- Congratulate yourself for identifying these thoughts and deciding you want to move on.

Most of the battle of getting over someone is getting over the habit.

Chapter 2

Getting Control Over Your Thoughts

Patternmaking is innately part of our development. Scientific texts refer to the way our brains record patterns as our autopilot or the subconscious[6,7]. In other words, the brain takes anything repetitive or resembling a routine and creates pathways in our mind to automate the process without needing further thought. We do this to preserve energy on critical thinking. We rarely forget how to walk or ride a bike because the brain stores it in its memory bank, automating that knowledge, so we don't have to relearn it again.

Think of it this way. If you stayed in a different hotel every night and went to a different place of work every day, you would tire out a good portion of your critical thinking energy by spending time every day familiarizing yourself with your new surroundings. When we get to the point where a pattern of activity has happened so many times, our

[6] Aryn, P. & West, R. 'The Conscious-Subconscious Interface: An Emerging Metaphor in HCI', *Proceedings of the Annual Meeting of the Cognitive Science Society*, 2001; 23(23) 2001. Accessed 14 February 2002: https://escholarship.org/uc/item/9z45z3x4

[7] Peters, S. *The Chimp Paradox* (Vermillion, 2012).

brain no longer needs new thoughts to carry it out. We automate it and move it into our subconscious or autopilot, where our body can carry out the process with little energy. This type of repetition forms habits, as in the famous experiment of Pavlov's dogs. Pavlov would ring a bell and then feed the dogs, ring a bell and feed the dogs. Over time the pattern became so automated in the dogs' brains that just ringing the bell would lead them to salivate.

In a similar way, we learn to be around people. Whether it is the person who sits on the desk next to us at work or gets on at the same train stop, we are creatures of habit. We learn other people's little movements, from their favourite coffee or sandwich, and create our own favourites, i.e. route to a shop, machine in the gym to chocolate flavour in a box. It's similar to how it takes energy and time to cut out a new path in a lawn of grass, but after a few times, the new route and path become clear. Automating patterns has helped us survive as a species in helping us learn to find food and water, note the movement of the seasons and the migration of animals, and never forget what poses a threat such as a particular plant or predator.

Most importantly, we can preserve vital headspace for issues that need new thought rather than meeting our basic survival requirements. You've probably experienced the same automation process on a familiar commute. I know I used to drive to work every day and arrive at the car park without really thinking about the route on the way at all. Once, when nipping to the shops on my day off, I found I had driven halfway to work accidentally. Hence, totally forgetting someone who has been part of your daily life definitely takes energy, as it's a new path and a new process for the brain to follow.

Understanding that a good portion of missing The Ex is just your brain yearning to return to an automated process or well-trodden path makes it easier to have more empathy for yourself. The way to speed your recovery from the breakup is to move your brain out of the recurring, familiar thinking pattern about The Ex and create a new thought pattern. This will take more mental energy, so you may have to be more conscious of what you're doing daily until this new path settles in your mind.

The brain will always remember the previous path and, due to the extra effort needed to create a new path, will often yearn to return to the ease of what was familiar. Your brain may somehow convince you that you miss The Ex, when really, you're missing that environment, where you knew what to expect. This habitual thinking can stop you from leaving a partner or even lead you to returning to someone who isn't good for you. You might doubt that the breakup was right or believe that the new way of life just doesn't feel right. But you need to ask what it is exactly that you're missing. Are you missing the person or the familiarity of the situation?

You might convince yourself that you want to return to a bad relationship when your brain really wants to return to what was easier and when it knew what to expect next, even when a new partner would be better for you.

Remind yourself that, for a little while, every day will feel more tiring because you're learning new patterns and habits, but once the new daily habits and patterns are more familiar, things will improve.

You want to move on, so even if your brain tries to tell you that this process is too daunting and you want to return to old habits, by keeping to your new routine and seeing results such as improvements in your mood and sleep, this inner resistance will lessen. Habits can take a while to form, but the more determined you are to put The Ex behind you and retrain your mind, the more your brain will get used to this new pattern. You may be experiencing brain fatigue during this time, and it can be helpful to remind yourself of the following:

- In the same way you learned to walk as a baby, by trying, falling down and trying again, not thinking of your Ex will just take a bit of practice. But your new life is here to stay. You will get used to this.

- Sit with any uncomfortable feelings and recognize them for what they are – minor fatigue from your new life. Do not use this feeling to convince yourself that you need to be back with the Ex.

- Remind yourself that the relationship broke up because it wasn't working, and even with discussions to fix it from time to time, it didn't change.

Training your brain to stay on the new path

I needed to rest more to allow my brain to embed my new routines and have the strength to keep making rational decisions. I needed to be kind to myself. Although being single meant I could go out more, being overtired meant I was more likely to be overemotional. So I often went to bed early, at least in the week, to give my brain the rest and relaxation it needed and to preserve my energy. Sometimes bed was a good option to switch off a bit. Having good rest even helped me to do better at work, which was an added bonus.

The constant fight to stop thinking about The Ex just deepened the thoughts about him. If I tell my brain to 'stop thinking of The Ex' I'm still thinking of The Ex, but now I'm constantly reminding myself not to think of him. That's like waking up every day saying 'don't eat chocolate';

surely it's better to think 'what shall I have for breakfast that is fulfilling' than to remind myself of food I should not have. As you can see, it diverts the brain to something practical that it can engage with. Not just an order to stop thinking of one thing, which really just reminds me repeatedly of said thing.

Like the analogy of a habit being a well-walked path, I couldn't just stop in my tracks. I needed to start to tread a new route.

I needed something new to think about and focus on to hijack my thinking. Friends said to try dating again; one way to get over one person is to date another. However, that wasn't a good idea as I wasn't in the right headspace. I needed a go-to list of superficial topics to bypass the momentary thoughts of The Ex, to prompt my brain to default to another issue, instead of telling it to just stop thinking. So I decided every time I found myself thinking about The Ex, I would write down a question.

If at work, I would make it work-related and have it ready for when my mind wandered. For example:

- Top three things to do today
- What needs to be done this hour, this morning, this afternoon?
- Think about a specific project or presentation

I also wanted to make sure I used my free time constructively. When I was at home, I often just zoned out by scrolling through my various social media feeds. But I liked putting pen to paper and thinking about constructive things for my daily life or writing notes to myself. It made me feel good. So my questions were things like:

- What can I do that I can look forward to today?
- What can I look forward to this week or end of this month?
- What things would make me more settled in my new temporary home?
- How will I make a vegan meal this week?
- What are my plans for this week? How can I make them more routine?

Questioning myself like this brought me back to the present moment and what I needed to do to feel better and move forwards. If outside work, I would text a friend and plan a night out, or do something constructive like going for a run, listening to an audio book or tidying up. At home, having a pen in hand, a pad, maybe a glass of wine, or even with the television on in the background; I felt much better writing than zoning out on my phone, constantly scrolling. There was also lesser risk of googling him with my phone not in my hand. So many positives from this one action. More importantly, my brain moved on from thinking about The Ex to my new world, a new positive day, and a routine without The Ex.

If your thoughts drift back to questions about your old relationship or The Ex, always forgive yourself. Then ask another question to change the topic in your brain.

Creating new passions to consume your thoughts

I also decided to start a new hobby, and, in one instance, it was gold. I decided to learn to play golf, so I needed to think about the kit, search for it on eBay and buy it (the clubs were not that expensive second-hand).

Even the notification on my phone from eBay that an auction was about to end was a delightful distraction instead of waiting for text messages from The Ex. And before long, I was heading off to a local driving range to practice.

I couldn't hit a donkey with a banjo, but I enjoyed doing something new, having somewhere to go and a conversation topic unrelated to The Ex or our breakup. I also started to look for friends to share my hobby with and new friends already in that world. Once a week, I'd head off to the range with my clubs, buy a bucket of balls, switch off my phone and enjoy my time alone (trying) to improve my swing. I even had dates at different driving ranges to keep things interesting. All positive actions that helped me and made me feel happier.

Accept the loss of a life planned out

While all these new positive thoughts filled me with hope, I couldn't picture where I'd be in six months. There was definitely a wonderful life without The Ex, but I didn't know what that would look like. I no longer had a life plan, and trying to formulate new plans felt impossible and unreal. My main thoughts were that I wanted to see more of my friends, and I needed somewhere longer term to live.

Without The Ex, I didn't have anyone to hang my plans on. I had so many options – almost too many. I could live anywhere. But so much choice just made me feel more lost. What did I want to do with my life? I could return to London and work there again. Where was I going to live? I moved in with my brother after the breakup, but I couldn't stay there forever. I couldn't work out if I wanted to stay, move to another part of the city or Country, or emigrate. I could stay with my brother or move closer to my childhood friends. On my own, I could afford much less. I'd likely rent rather than buy, as my plans could change again if I met someone, so there was no point buying somewhere now. Or maybe I could buy. I am an independent woman. I can own my own home and do it up. But where? How long will that take to save up for – years, decades?

I needed to sit down with myself and get all this straight. It was like, before the breakup, I had the boyfriend/husband part ticked off as done, and now I was starting again. Looking for someone to share my life and have a family with. The few years with The Ex I had classed as a task achieved. *Well done me, job done, got a boyfriend and committed relationship, next stop kids and marriage or marriage and kids.* No pressure, except for this unwritten expectation. I didn't know the finer details, but I thought I'd be with The Ex. My brain was exhausted, so I decided to just get the answers for this week, this month, this season, and worry about the long-term plan later. I told myself, *I don't have to do anything about this now, today or this week. I don't need an answer on my long-term plan. I don't need a solution. There is very unlikely a sudden fix. If I get through today well, today becomes a week going well, which becomes a month, then I find one day I haven't thought about The Ex in some time.*

The big picture stuff can feel scary, so focus on the little stuff and short-term. Maybe not the next two years but plans to get through the next couple of seasons.

Enjoy every day and set some goals

When you're hurting, having something to focus on can be helpful. I decided to focus on my birthday in three months. Then I got out a pad and a pen and asked:

- What would be amazing to do this year and amazing to achieve?
- What would be fun and give me something to look forward to?
- What will keep me busy doing things in the meantime?

I started to write out a list of things I knew I wanted to do, like run the local half-marathon and go on an overseas holiday. I didn't want my list to be too challenging. I also didn't want it to be so easy that it wasn't worthwhile. I decided to set a handful of challenges to complete over the next 12 months. My list included some fun and new stuff, adventures, and places I'd never visited. It looked like this:

- Run a half-marathon.
- Go on a girls' holiday.
- Learn to make cocktails.
- Climb a mountain.
- Go to Scotland.
- Eat food I have never tried before.
- Try a new drink.
- Do an extreme run.
- Try a new sport.
- Learn (or at least try) a new language.
- Cook a new meal from scratch. (The Ex always said I was a bit of a useless cook, and even though I cooked a good proportion of our meals, he said I was never really experimental.)

- Finish my photo books of trips I have taken (so I can reminisce about just how good my life can be with happy times).

I posted my challenge list on my social media feed, inviting friends to offer more ideas. My friend, Dee, responded within seconds that I should spend the day in a squirrel suit. That made me chuckle. It was working already. Not that I would dress as a squirrel, but at least it was a new idea. When I drifted off in my head about The Ex, I used to bring my mind back to my challenge list.

Planning new challenges will pass the time, keep you motivated and help you move on.

In a nutshell

- Be kind to yourself and remember that much of you missing The Ex is missing the habits and patterns of being with them. Once the habits of thinking about them dwindle, things will improve.
- You can speed this along by training your mind and creating new routines. Your mind will want to return to old familiar ways (of thinking about The Ex), but kindly returning your thoughts to your new patterns will help you get more used to life without them.
- Focusing on new passions, new things to look forward to and be involved in can fill your time and help you move on.
- Often the loss of the plans you had with The Ex can be the most hurtful, as you can find yourself unsure of what will happen next for you. You may want to have big milestones in your future already sorted out, and the path to these is less clear now you're single. Do not worry about this now. This will come. Focus on the days, and the months and years will fall into place.
- Accept that you won't have all the answers now but start with small goals as you work out the next stages of your life.

Get your notebook out

- Think about times you were distracted by thoughts of The Ex. Typically, when or where does this happen? when is it the most emotive. Think of patterns which may evoke this where you can prevent this from starting, e.g. put on a happy song when you wake, do not have your phone in your hand to prevent scrolling or visiting their social media. List these preventative ideas that can help you stay productive.
- When you're distracted by these thoughts at work, create a list of your immediate highest priorities that you need to achieve. Write this list big and bold, put it front and centre, if your mind wanders bring it back to the task written on the desk.
- Add positive thought prompts to your day to keep you on track. You may start a new self-care routine, try new recipes, visit new places or take a walk at lunch time.
- What hobbies or events can you participate in, volunteer or train for? This could fill your time and help refocus your thoughts. Some ideas are:
    - decorating a new kitchen, getting new kitchen equipment to try
    - things you did when you were younger, such as sports, hobbies
    - list of top films/series to watch, and self-development or relaxing books to read
    - find motivational leaders to watch on YouTube or TikTok
- You can keep yourself motivated by listing some challenges for now or this year, from huge things like travel to smaller things like reading a new book. Plan when to make these happen.

I want to run away,
but everywhere I go,
I am there.

Chapter 3

Address Poor Self-talk

You may find that you spend much of your day asking yourself some horrid questions in your head and hurting your own feelings with negative self-talk, which may go something like this:

I bet he's met someone. No doubt he cheated on me. He probably went off me a while ago. I'm not exactly pretty. I have put on a bit of weight lately. I think I'm funny, but other girls are quirkier and funnier. Other girls are cleverer and more successful than I am. I'm just not going to meet anyone. Loving me is just too hard. There is just nothing special about me. Look at her. She's really pretty. I bet he would fancy her. Maybe I was boring in bed. Maybe he just got bored of me and wanted someone more interesting.

I would ask myself questions in my head, such as:

- Why has this happened to me?
- Will I ever meet anyone?
- Am I just unlovable?

- Did he ever love me?
- Was there someone else?
- Am I ugly?
- Am I horrible once people get to know me?
- Will I ever have children?
- Will I end up alone for good?
- Am I better off just being alone?
- Why is he OK and I'm a mess?
- How could he let this happen?
- Why doesn't The Ex love me anymore?
- Why doesn't he try and get me back?

Being your own best friend

This kind of thinking quickly leads to low mood and even depression. If you had a friend or colleague saying this stuff in your ear all day or texting you incessant, negative, soul-destroying drivel, you would tell them to go away, work at another desk or even office, ignore their texts and not take their calls.

I was talking to myself like this all the time. *Why would he want to be with someone who thought so low of herself! Jeepers, even that is more negative self-talk.* The worst thing is these thoughts started cycling around my brain – the same questions and statements. I would zone off into a negative cycle, distracting myself from positive actions and neglecting myself. My brain wasn't a nice place to be. I felt trapped, like I had a large dark rock sitting on my chest. It was hard to breathe for the negative thoughts, sentencing and questioning of what had happened and what was going to happen next. Finally, I told my brain, *Enough is enough, brain. I'm tired of thinking these same thoughts.*

My plan was to take each of the questions, think about it just once, document the answer for future reference and draw a line under it. I knew once I had resolved the thought, then if I started to think about it again, I could stop myself in my tracks, refer to my answers and stop the cycle of negative self-talk.

The key to this process was identifying the thoughts, holding them out in the daylight as the poisonous little creatures they were and banishing them by actively choosing to correct assumptions and negativity behind the thought rather than just try not to think about it. This exercise (or exorcism) made it easier to identify the thoughts and stop them in their tracks.

When you process your thoughts category by category, deal with them and then file them away, you can start to pick out a folder or category of thoughts and replace them with new ones. More positive, kinder thoughts that make you feel excited about your future gains rather than depressed about past perceived losses.

Replacing negative thoughts with positive, helpful comments that you'd get from your best friend will make you feel more at home and welcome in your headspace.

For this practice, you need a pen and paper to write down all your questions about The Ex or even general negative thoughts you are having about yourself. Then, act as if your best friend were writing the response underneath. Don't think about what you're going to write. Just note down the questions as they appear in your mind. You might want to use a different coloured pen for the answers but write from your best friend's perspective, write the answer as a person who wants to help you. See what response the best friend within you comes out with.

When I did this process, I sat and looked at the blank page and the black ballpoint pen I was holding. I wrote down the first questions that came into my head. I then read each question as if a best friend had written me a letter, a friend that I loved and loved me. I pictured my best friend and visualized this beautiful soul going through this breakup instead of me. I visualized what I would say to her if she were having these thoughts, asking herself these questions, and I started to write a reply. These are the questions and responses that I recorded using this practice.

If a friend talked to me how I talk to myself, I'd never speak to them again.

Why has this happened to me?

Response: Nothing has happened to you personally. Your relationship ended and I know you are hurting so much. Sometimes relationships don't work out. It happens to pretty much everyone at some time; although it feels like you're on your own in this and that other people are in relationships, it's not just you. Royalty and celebrities are not immune to breakups. Remember that a relationship ending doesn't make either of you bad people or that you have failed. It's just unfortunately the case that breakups happen every day. Some people spend 20, 30, 40 years together and then break up. They break up after marriage, they break up after kids, and they even break up after retirement. Why do you think so many successful songs are written about heartbreak? Relationship breakdowns happened before you were born and will continue to occur after you die. Relationships break down. It's a fact. This isn't just you. Everyone goes through it. You are a regular person going through a hurtful life experience.

How did this happen?

Response: You admitted that you two weren't happy. You'd already talked to The Ex about how things had changed. Life just got in the way. He is probably trying to work it out as much as you are. He wasn't happy. You were unhappy. You'd started to argue over little things. He'd started to ignore you. You'd started to ignore him. You split up because being together no longer made you happy or being together made you much sadder than was healthy, and it was time for the relationship to end.

Why is he OK and I'm a mess?

Response: First, you don't know anything about how The Ex is doing. Just because he hasn't tried to get you back and isn't messaging doesn't mean he is OK or perfectly fine. You aren't messaging him either. So, is this statement true? The reality is you don't know how The Ex is doing. He may not be fine at all. Second, are you ***not*** doing fine? You have friends, you have somewhere to stay, you have a job – if you stopped being so distracted and sitting in this negative thought pattern, you'd be doing even better. You are not a mess. You are sad about this and that is OK. You will be fine. It's the sad, miserable habits that are causing your problems.

So why am I sad?

Response: The end of a relationship is sad, and it's OK to be sad about it. But constantly asking yourself these horrid questions is making you sad. The answers you're giving yourself are untrue and make you feel worse. Again, this cycle makes you sad rather than the breakup itself. You didn't get on with The Ex at the end. You two started to move into quite a negative, toxic space emotionally. This breakup is, therefore, a good thing. Be sad a little bit. The end of a relationship is sad. You meant a lot to each other at the start, and things have changed. The relationship turned sour, which is common when you spend more time together, and you both change. Don't stay sad too long; some of this sadness is simply your choice.

Will I ever meet someone?

Response: Are you the only person to have ever split up with someone? No. When you're ready, you will get out there, start dating, meet many guys who would be good partners, and you will fall for one and be in love again. You know of people in retirement who have met new partners and gotten married. Your widowed grandmother met an elderly gentleman in her 70s and moved in with him. This relationship wasn't meant for you long term. You are now free to find a partner who is a better fit – better still, you might meet the partner of your dreams! Anything can happen, but you aren't going to find your next partner getting upset and in the dumps over an Ex that made you unhappy.

Why am I single?

Response: You are single because you felt a lot for The Ex, but that was at the start of your relationship. Over time you grew apart, you changed, and how you both felt for each other changed. You felt less in love and less happy. You both tried to bring the relationship back to a better place (I think you more than him), but you haven't been able to get it there. As a result, you've freed yourself to look for a better match. Is it better to be in a relationship and unhappy than single and available when a great potential match comes along? Why do you see the end of an unhappy relationship as a failure? It's a success. You have successfully tried out a relationship that didn't work. You are looking for one that suits you better. If an old coat didn't fit anymore, would you see it as a failure not to wear it? No, you take it off and find one that is a better fit.

Why do all my relationships seem to fail?

Response: You've had a few relationships. You've also grown and changed a lot in recent years. Some of the relationships have ended due to circumstances, and others were a bad fit. There is nothing wrong with you. You are not mean, cruel, unkind, unlovable. Everyone is lovable by someone. There are 7.7 billion people in the world. If half of those are male (and you ignore the children and elderly), there are a few billion males on the planet. The small number you have met, dated and had a relationship with is a minuscule fraction. No one is unlovable. Let's face it, even murderers on death row have women fall in love with them and write to them. Would you rather have had one toxic relationship from age 16 and stayed in it? No. You are proof that you and The Ex want more from life. This breakup is a successful indicator that you want great happiness in your life.

If things were not right, why does this feel so wrong?

Response: You miss The Ex because you loved him. However, I don't think you love him anymore. You miss The Ex because he was funny at the start, but you haven't laughed together in a long time. You miss The

Ex because he was safe. You were in a relationship, and now you're not. The direction of your life is unknown, which feels a bit scary. You want to have children one day, and with The Ex, that could have happened. Now you're worrying yourself about whether you will meet someone, if you will marry or if you will have children. But these life events are not related to The Ex. You can share those things with someone else.

There are the times you both shared that you will look back on with sorrow and a little pain, but surely spending the rest of your life with someone because you were too scared to be alone is not a reason to share that life. You know, towards the end, you didn't bring the best out of each other. You didn't build each other up or stand by each other. At one time, you loved each other, but not for a long time.

So, in summary, you miss him, but you don't miss your relationship with him.

Feeling better

Once you've worked through your questions, you'll feel better about the breakup. You might even want to keep your answers with you in case you start cycling through old thoughts. Getting this out of my head and onto paper was so useful. I would pull out my page of questions and answers whenever my thoughts started to cycle back to the past. Reading through the responses would remind my rational brain of why I shouldn't get back together with The Ex. On the days I didn't have my notepad, I would get in a tizzy. I would want him back and get upset. I would beat myself up with thoughts that I was useless, ugly, uninteresting, not good enough on so many levels.

Once I looked at my question-and-answer notes, I would remember there wasn't anything to go back to. I would use the answers I had documented to give me the real reason why the relationship hadn't worked out and had to end. This was the rational reason. We were both better off finding someone new.

Asking better questions

Hopefully what you wrote to yourself is so much more positive than what you've been saying in your own head. So now that you're feeling better after this pep talk, what do you do?

I didn't actually know what to think about. All I knew was that there were so many possibilities without The Ex. I had been asking myself so many fearful questions but it was time to ask some more positive ones:

- How can I be kinder to myself today and this week?
- What can I say to myself to make myself feel better?
- What wonderful things can happen for me now?

All these wonderful thoughts entered my head. With the next partner, I wanted to feel like we had the most special bond. I dreamed of weekends away hill-climbing and being surprised with treats and birthday dinners. I felt excited about meeting someone who would support me and make me feel like I could do anything. I wasn't sure if I would find these things in my next partner, but I had these colourful laughing thoughts which made me feel relaxed and that my destiny was safe. I also knew I was free to go anywhere and could travel for six months if I chose – Peru, Australia, Canada – and that I could live anywhere (visas pending).

The personal development coach Tony Robbins clearly states that 'what you think is what you feel'. I had been thinking horrid depressing thoughts, and as a result, I had been feeling horrid depressing feelings. I was ready to think and feel a different way.

Letting the thoughts go

Another solution to this daily mental battle is to accept The Ex's presence in your mind. This internal fight to stop thinking and wondering is exhausting. So, welcome The Ex to use your head as their own rent-free personal flat, tell them to make themselves a cuppa and, as always, forget to put their dirty laundry in the basket. Stay in there, safe in the knowledge that The Ex will vanish with time and, in the meantime, get on with your day.

I knew if I stopped fighting myself and simply accepted The Ex would be hanging out in my head all day, then the infighting would stop. I knew my mental battle would become less of a struggle with time. Especially as this was a mental battle he would never know about, or even, in real life, be a part of.

I would get into a new pattern of things to think about, and then this thinking would disappear – become a ghost. This was very different to telling myself to stop thinking of him. As I described in Chapter 2, I would distract myself with simple questions, but I would also simply focus on something else. But sometimes, when it was all just a little too much, I just figured if The Ex was going to be there, so be it – I would not fight with myself. As long as I didn't think anything negative, I'd just let the thoughts and memories go.

Remembering reality

You may find that some thoughts about The Ex make you really sad. For me, it wasn't having someone to come home to. The Ex was a big part of my everyday life. If my boss moaned, I called him. If the Peking duck with pancakes was on sale in the local supermarket, he would call me. (One week it was on offer, and I bought five, and we couldn't face it again for six months.) There wasn't a thought we generally didn't share. It seemed weird not to have him to talk to.

I remember my friend Lyn calling to tell me about her dad being ill. She told me how lucky I was to have someone at home to turn to. Being single, she just wanted someone to give her a hug, cook her dinner and tell her it would all be OK. A few days before, I had been under a lot of pressure at work and revising for exams in the evening. After a long day, I came home hoping for some sympathy to find The Boyfriend in a foul mood and his dirty underwear strewn over my revision notes. I went downstairs to ask him to put his dirty laundry in the basket. His throwback was that I was in a foul mood and just trying to have a row over nothing. I'd described the scenario to Lyn and said if I were single, at least my notes would be minus the dirty pants, and I'd come home to an empty house, not a moody boyfriend. She laughed and agreed that what she wanted was the ideal, not the reality.

So when I wanted to stop missing The Ex, I found it helpful to remember the relationship for what it was – the bad times, not just the good ones. Don't get me wrong, I don't think you should let The Ex become a monster in your mind and forget all the good stuff. However, remembering the good times and memories may make you cry, while remembering the stuff which annoyed you will help you get through the day and help you move on mentally to find the right partner.

The bigger picture – keeping perspective

I knew I had a good life, and although it wasn't ideal, I was lucky to be able to live with my brother and his wife at short notice. Just because I had faced a setback in one area of my life didn't mean that everything else needed to be viewed negatively. I had been busy throwing away all the great things I had achieved, everything I still had and everything I had to look forward to just because this one element of my life, The Ex, had gone. So I pulled out my journal and started to focus on the positives:

- Just because I am single doesn't mean that one day I won't get married to the man of my dreams and have children.
- Just because I am living with my brother now doesn't mean that I won't have my dream house later in life and have everything I have ever wanted in that home. I'm not talking about a Beyonce-style mansion, but a lovely home that makes me happy and houses my little family.
- Just because I have broken up with one person doesn't mean there's no one for me. It was one person in a world of billions of men. I can find another partner.
- Just because I have been sad about this part of my life's experience, it doesn't mean I won't have such wonderful blessings to come, a wonderful life and journey to share with my future children and partner.

I kept thinking that because I had split from The Ex, I was somehow no good. I was unlovable. I spent a few moments acknowledging how many people loved me – my parents, my brother, my friends and people I had met at school and work. I had so many wonderful stories and great experiences and will continue to have a great life. I knew I couldn't keep wasting that potential by being sad about this one person. I assigned so much meaning to the rejection I felt from the break. I needed to disconnect from it – and The Ex.

In a nutshell

- Be your own best friend, not your worst enemy. Don't say horrible things to yourself that you wouldn't say to someone else. The time after the breakup can be made more hurtful by the questions your mind asks itself.
- Use that best friend voice within to create more empathy for yourself when you're feeling stuck and use it to gain clarity on those nagging questions.
- Keep your notes with you to refer back to your positive thinking when you are feeling low.
- Ultimately The Ex is going to be on your mind, so don't beat yourself up about it. Find ways to be more caring to yourself.
- Remind yourself of some bad times when things weren't all rosy, and remember the breakup was needed to allow you to meet someone new.
- Just because this one element is not going how you wished, there are so many other things going so well for you. Remember all of your blessings and things to be grateful for. Celebrate the positives and past wins.

Get your notebook out

- Write down the thoughts you're struggling with and all the negative statements you're saying to yourself. Now imagine your own best friend was saying these to herself. Someone that you love and someone who also loves you dearly.
- Write down all the questions you keep asking yourself. The questions you really want to have the answer to. Leave a space under each one.
- Now, imagine that your best friend has written these to you. That their heart is breaking. Answer each one of these questions as if that best friend was in your predicament.
- Look at the phrasing of your answers. Have you been as forgiving in your own mind? Have you talked to yourself kindly?
- Write down the reality of the relationship, the times that really got you down or let you down. It can help to remember the reality of the relationship, not just the good.
- Now write down some positive questions you want to ask yourself. For example: How can I be kinder to myself today and this week? What can I say to myself to make myself feel better? What wonderful things can happen for me now?
- What are you grateful for, what great things do you have in your life?

First, we make our habits, and then our habits make us.

—John Dryden

Chapter 4

Your Environment and Routine

Following a breakup, life has two definitive characteristics. The first is that life is very different every day, the other is that although it is different, every day ***feels*** the same.

For me, there were so many changes. Apart from not seeing The Ex, I was living somewhere new, commuting a different route to work, seeing my friends more, and staying over at friends' houses (which I never did for some reason in the relationship). I wasn't just seeing old friends but making new ones. I was also eating different food, maybe because I wasn't at home for mealtimes anymore or because I didn't bother making an effort to eat. But every day also felt like Groundhog Day. I was just existing, passing the time. Weirdly, I appeared to be counting the days since the breakup. Just sitting it out until the pain and the sickness of my broken heart passed. Every day I woke at 3 a.m. I researched it and read that when your body is in shock, you can wake up in the middle of the night. I lost hair. Apparently, it's really common.

Every day I woke up with fresh air across my face. Then the sick feeling came, the realization that I was desperately missing something. The energy and motivation to get up drained into the floor, like someone had turned on a tap in my stomach and emptied out any last drips of happiness. I'd look at the clock; it's 7 a.m. *Not bad,* I'd think to myself, *at least I fell back to sleep after the 3 a.m. wake-up*. I'd turn on my stereo and press play on the playlist I'd been listening to over the last month: John Mayer or other slow, mellow, sad songs. I'd shower then slump on the bed, exhausted, before dragging myself to work.

After another unproductive day at work, trying to focus and keep busy, I'd drive home, eat something on toast, watch television. When my sister-in-law and brother came home, we'd make small conversation while they looked worriedly at me, not least over how much weight I'd lost. My brother would ask about my day. I would ask about his. He'd offer me a cup of tea; I'd decline and decide to go to bed.

Tick, another day survived.

I knew this was no way to carry on – just existing. I knew this frame of mind would set me up to fail every day. As soon as the thought entered my head in the morning, the reminder I had split from The Ex, that moment dictated the rest of my day. My body was slumped when I woke up. Fuelled by sad music and poor nutrition, my energy sank lower through the day. Slump by slump, I was dictating and designing a sad and existing state.

Changing behaviours instigates change

Change happens when our behaviours change. After all, does a happy, motivated person get up in a slump? Do they ignore their hunger, not make an effort to dress or shower? The fact is, no, they don't. How you hold your body tells your brain how you feel. How you feel then impacts your body. When you think motivational thoughts, the body doesn't ache so much from the pain of sadness.

I knew feeling this miserable wasn't good for me, that I was doing this to myself. I even knew the science behind the body/mind link from Tony Robbins. Our emotions, thoughts and body movements are all joined. If you think sad things, you will start to feel sad emotions, your body will move in a sad way, which will make you feel sad. It's a cycle, and just like that, you *are* sad. So thinking happy thoughts leads to happy emotions and movements. The body can be tricked into believing it is happy and run the cycle the other way. Fed up with Groundhog Day, I decided to hold my body and move like a happy person, and focus on happy thoughts. In time, I knew I would feel happier emotions and *be* happy.

I couldn't change my first thought of missing The Ex, no more than I could stop my subconscious from waking me up at 3 a.m. But I did have control over every other minute of the day. I knew it would take some mental training, but I was determined that my first waking minute would no longer ruin the other 1,439 minutes in the day. If you had £1,440 and dropped £1 – you wouldn't throw the other £1,439 in the bin. You'd decide how to spend it well. I needed to redesign my time, my days, the same way. And this is how I did it.

The purge

When I moved out of The Ex's, I left anything I didn't need that had big memories or big emotional anchors, including:

- All paper copies of photos (emptying any frames).
- The slow cooker that we used to make many happy meals.

- Christmas tree decorations (but I took the tree).
- Birthday cards and old gifts, especially anything cute from when we first got together.

Following my moving out, I also:

- Donated casual clothes I wore at home and bought all new fresh casual clothes cheaply.
- Went from brunette to dark blonde, long hair to a short bob.
- Bought a new swimming costume.
- As daft as it sounds, I even changed my slippers and comfy night socks. It was like they were tainted.

Thankfully I had spare pillows and bedding from when I lived on my own before The Ex. I think I would have redecorated the whole house had I been in the same house, and The Ex was one leaving.

New healthy daily behaviours

In resetting behaviours, the first thing is to design what that day will look like when you wake up. Take a notebook and pen, and think about how you'll get up, prepare for the day ahead, how you'll move, what you'll do and any triggers that might commonly derail you and what you'll do instead. Think about how your movements throughout the day can lift you up. Maybe that nice breakfast you're going to start the day with, the flask you will buy so you can have hot chocolate on the move. The movie you've picked out for yourself. If you're derailed by thoughts about The Ex, spend a few minutes at the end of the day with a notepad and pen. Note down what happened and how this could be avoided in future by adding in a new routine or more self-love.

A happy, healthy environment

I looked around my messy room and saw dirty clothes lying in small piles in the corners and on the furniture, and most of my belongings still in bags. I needed to tidy up – orderly room, orderly mind. I started by creating an environment where I could feel happy and settled as soon as I woke or came home.

Since the breakup, I had been spending a long time every day just sitting on my bed after waking up, staring off into space. I couldn't even blame my phone for that one. I just sat there dreading starting the day, wasting time, making myself late to work, and not even using the time to get ready and look presentable. My first step then, before I even allowed myself to think of anything, was to get up and shower.

After my shower, I got ready in front of the mirror. I'd already sorted through my clothes and matched a few outfits. I'd carefully choose an outfit for the day – work trousers, a nice blouse. Even better, I made sure they were clean. I had gotten into the habit of picking up clothes from a couple of days ago, thinking they were clean only to find a dirty mark. I unpacked my high heels. Time to start wearing different shoes, not the same worn out and messy looking flats every day. Stylish footwear always makes me feel better instantly. All my makeup and hair products were unpacked properly, and I knew starting the day better styled and better dressed ***had*** to impact my mood for the day. I was off to a good start.

I placed a photo of my best friend where I could see it. I still had a few empty photo frames which used to have photos of The Ex and me; I replaced these with happy photos of me with friends and put them around my room.

Don't let yourself down. In that first minute, you have a better chance of all the other minutes falling into line. You've got to start the day better.

Find a better soundtrack

I'd been listening to sad mellow breakup music when I woke up, and it had become the soundtrack for the rest of my day. Sad music doesn't just make me think of sad words and situations, but I sing along, aligning my brain to sadness. I needed a better soundtrack, uplifting songs to kick me into tapping the steering wheel or wiggling my shoulders in a car dance.

I started to pull out old playlists, ones I used to listen to in my late teens. Happy memories of when I felt independent, happy, strong, when I had friends and a six-week summer of joy ahead of me. The first song was Calvin Harris. I started to sing along, then dance a little. I didn't feel the need to cry. Right. I needed to start listening to happy songs from now on.

I had been single until I was in my early 20s. I was one of those girls who had many male mates but never dated anyone. Those days were my happiest times. Sitting in the sixth form, playing darts. We had such geeky humour. I used to wear boyish jeans and a t-shirt. I was one of the lads, joking away in physics. I was the only girl in the class and took to the challenge well. Writing random statements on each other's lab coats and joining in the banter because two of the lads fancied the chemistry teacher. I laughed at myself. Things seemed so much simpler then. I didn't feel the biological clock ticking or pressure to meet someone. When did It all become so serious?

I planned on asking a few friends about the music they listened to, happy stuff I could add to my playlist. It also proved a distracting conversation topic, which wasn't about The Ex.

I loaded the playlist to put in the car. I threw in tunes from every happy era in my life: Lionel Richie's *Dancing on the Ceiling*, Phil Collins' *Going Loco*, Madonna's dance hits. Oldies but goodies. Calvin Harris – pretty much every song he's ever made has been a happy dance track, so they were all pretty safe to download. I needed to have better days if I wanted to feel better. Step one was stopping doing things that made me feel sad. Blasting out the songs, I felt very different getting ready, and I looked better.

Scents bring positive thoughts

Not only does music transport us to another time, but so do scents. The laundry products my parents use, the room freshener at my best friend's house, the perfume an old school friend used to wear, which was so strong I could smell her before I saw her. I'd always worn the same two scents when I'd been with The Ex and I knew that had to change. I needed to be new and fresh, so I needed a new scent. I packed away my more recent perfumes in a bag at the bottom of my wardrobe and hunted for a new one I'd received as a Christmas gift and used that instead.

Move your body with confidence

Feeling better – showering and dressing nicely –also made me feel more confident, so I began to hold myself better.

I bought some new clothes to help me feel confident in my body. I didn't have much money, so I made a rule: if I wasn't excited to wear the outfit immediately, I didn't buy it. That way, everything new I wore made me feel amazing. Not clothes I knew would look better with fewer kilos on my hips and tummy but thought I should get because I'd found them on the sale racks.

I needed to stop moving around as if I were sitting under a rain cloud and move my body like someone that's just signed a £2 million record deal. I'm not saying that I started walking around with a mobile phone strapped to my ear, yelling, 'Buy, buy, buy, sell, sell, sell,' but I needed to stop walking to my desk as if I was worried about being detected and sprayed with insect killer.

Since the split, I had tried to hide as much as possible because I looked like a mess. My work had also fallen behind because I'd been avoiding face-to-face discussions necessary to getting things done. This needed to stop. I told myself, *I am awesome at my job. I need to be presentable and start to be seen again, looking good, looking happy and most importantly, progressing the work.*

Take baby steps. Start by looking good and moving more confidently around colleagues. Don't be afraid to be seen.

In a nutshell

- When you're hurting from a breakup, you can get into a rut, whereby your routine and environment enable the negative feelings from the breakup to last longer than they need to, or you want to. This can include the music you listen to or the perfumes that you wear.
- You feel negative, so you don't do anything about your environment, but your environment encourages you to feel negative, making you feel stuck.
- Reset your surroundings to trigger a better start to your day by creating a happy environment, changing the soundtrack, investing in plenty of self-care and walking tall.
- Tidy your room or home, clean your clothes and arrange these well, making it easier to dress to look good. Go through your wardrobe and set out clothes that make you feel good about yourself and remove those that do not make you feel confident. Potentially buy new items which you feel great in immediately. Put up pictures of good times with good friends or family.
- Avoid songs with depressing, sad or longing words or sounds. Switch off music that you listened to with The Ex or that reminds you of The Ex. Play happy music and look for new artists. Switch on songs from your past that you associate with really good times.
- The more you lack self-care, the more you will feel like a mess and feel sad. Set up good daily routines that make you feel nourished and loved.
- Move your body with confidence to encourage your body to feel happier.

Get your notebook out

- Write out your current daily routine, look at what you have written about your day; how can you take opportunities to improve feeling good? Consider what you wear, what you eat, how often you shower or take a hot relaxing bath, when you can take a walk during your work day.
- Your home and work environment can improve your mood and thoughts, this can aid in your feeling more settled and relaxed. Move things around to make your daily routine easier. Declutter areas of your home, pull out some cheerful pictures or photos.
- What music do you listen to and what TV programmes/movies you watch? Are these bringing you down? Can you put on something more fun and happier?
- Think about how you move your body or sit. Can you move your body more confidently to improve how you feel? How you feel is how you think.

Contacting The Ex will not bring closure. The best closure is simply moving on.

Chapter 5

To Contact or Not Contact The Ex

I knew that there was a lot of science around habits and behaviours. There have been thousands of research papers from universities worldwide, published in scientific journals from health psychology to industry. Research from University College London reports that habits form within a range, with the average being 66 days[8,9]. I know the longer I went without contacting The Ex and distracted myself, the better I felt. I knew, in time, I would feel good. I just needed to train my brain to faze him out and focus on my current life. When my mind drifted into looking for ways to attain information on him or wanting to contact him, I brought it back to my current priorities. The longer I limited contact and got out of the habit of speaking to him, the harder my brain worked to get a kick from other things in my life, and he lost that chemical power over me.

---

[8] Lally, P. van Jaarsveld, C, Potts, H. & Wardle, J. `How are habits formed: Modelling habit formation in the real world`. *European Journal of Social Psychology, 40,* 998-1009. 2010

[9] Gardner, B. `Making health habitual: the psychology of 'habit-formation' and general practice`. Gen Pract. 62(605): 664–666. 2012

I didn't want to log the days since the split, as that was another way to think of him, but I did say to myself: Three months from now, life will be better, but only while I don't have any contact with The Ex. If we are in contact, then the clock starts again.

The initial days were slow, and I rarely felt good. But as the days passed and I looked forward, it felt more positive. If I stayed in contact with The Ex they may share more information than I need to or want to know, they may also share things they know would sting my ego or heart.

From time to time, you might hear from The Ex or wish to contact them. It is worth planning out in advance what you will do if you have the urge to contact them or they contact you.

Timing

I already knew it wasn't a good idea to call or message The Ex when I'd been out drinking. After a few Proseccos, I was more inclined to say things I would regret, not follow the conversation properly, not remember much of the conversation and not end it saying the things I really wanted to say. That is obvious; don't start a conversation when drunk. However, it also ruined my night because it would totally engulf my thoughts which would overtake the evening mentally, meaning that the friend or friends I was out with would get a crappy deal. I wouldn't be fully in the room with them, because I'd be checking my phone, thinking of responses, rereading his messages, writing a long response, reading it through, adding bits, removing bits. If I was inclined to, I might ask my friends about it, what they thought of my response and so on. Night ruined.

So when you're out, don't message them. If they message you, either leave it to the morning or just say, 'I'm really sorry, I can't reply properly at the moment. I would love to chat but better to do this tomorrow. I hope that's OK.' Then just best to leave it. It's respectful and suggests you're happy to have a conversation rather than playing games. Come tomorrow, they may wish to play games and feel affronted. But at least your mind is clearer, and if you follow up the conversation the next day, it is more likely to be a quality interaction, and you won't have ruined your night out.

Never call or text when you're out. You won't be thinking straight, and it will distract you from the good times in front of you.

Don't be fooled by your brain

What I didn't realize was my brain had an array of tools to convince me it was a good idea to message The Ex. It's like your brain saying to eat chocolate – lying to you that this is a great idea as you're going to work it off later, that this is lower calorie chocolate or you can just eat a little, even though you know full well you will consume the lot and that you aren't going to feel like that exercise later. My brain lies. So here are all the brain tricks to avoid.

I am over him, but I really want to be friends

My brain would say: I think we can be friends. It's such a shame after being so close that we don't even speak. How sad. We can at least keep in contact. I shall contact him – clearly as a friend, to try and maintain that relationship – right now.

What I learned to tell myself: Nope. Some people, some very special people, can do this. I know that I can't maintain a relationship with The

Ex when I want to be with them myself. I am the type to get jealous, and I am not really over him. Just because I feel good today doesn't mean that I am over him and ready to be friends tomorrow or next week.

Would you go for a coffee with The Ex if you met the love of your life? Would you invite them to your wedding? If not, why try to stay friends?

Any closeness we share would be confusing because we weren't friends before we started dating. There is no reason why we would go back to being friends after. If I got a new boyfriend, would I still want to hang out with him? Nope! Would my boyfriend like it? Nope. When he gets a new girlfriend, would I expect him and the new girlfriend to meet for coffee? Nope.

Your brain is tricking you. Because as you already know, it wants information on them and time with them, because that's what your brain is used to. When your brain gets what it's craving, it gets a hit of serotonin, oxytocin and even endorphins, which makes you feel good. That is all this is. If in a year from now when you aren't thinking of them at all, you happen to see him and you become friends, fine. But this isn't a friend. This was a boyfriend or girlfriend, and now it is over, and you have to accept that.

Wanting to ask burning questions

My brain would say: I need to ask him a burning question as he will know the answer. I have seen this thing that he loves which is on offer, this play that he loves is in town or a film we had wanted to watch is in the cinema. I need to tell/ask him now.

What I learned to tell myself: Nope. This is your brain reaching out for familiar patterns and a hit of hormones to hear from him. When you were together, this kneejerk reaction is the sharing in the relationship. You were thinking of them, and this is how you showed you loved/cared for them. But sending a message of this type after the breakup will likely end in a thank you – they will simply give the answer or not respond at all.

Also, I had to ask myself what response I wanted. Would I be happy with a simple thank you? I would think it over, and yes, I would, but then I would wonder how he was doing and maybe expect him to ask me how I am. What would I put back? Probably 'Yeah, good, thanks.' So that isn't a conversation, is it? So why send the first message if I don't have a plan for the interaction that may or may not follow? This is all habit, I just want to contact him, but it won't help me. I doubt it will help The Ex either. So, no point informing them of little things you used to share together when you were with them.

I am feeling so low, did he ever love me?

My brain would say: I need to know if he ever loved me. Did I even mean anything at all?

What I learned to tell myself: Nope. This one is the worst. After a breakup, this is such an easy pit to fall into. Desperate for information and spinning about why the relationship went wrong, you think the only person who can answer this question is The Ex, but that isn't true.

Reaching out for reassurance from The Ex is the worst idea by far because sending out this message would only have one outcome, which is going to make you feel a million times worse. Surely it could go well, you might think. No. Because:

- You are broken up, regardless of whether they ever loved you. You are split up now, and there is a reason for it.
- They could tell you they never loved you purely because they are mad at you, they're hurting, they're in a bad mood, or they just want to be spiteful.

You know the answer. They loved you once and may love you now, but you're not compatible. I don't believe it's possible to fake it all. So I already know the answer to this question. I don't need to ask. Again, it's my brain wanting to go to him for familiarity when I am feeling low. Also, just because he loved me doesn't mean that was how I needed to be loved. I needed someone to be on my team. I didn't feel we were a team.

So if I messaged The Ex and said, 'I miss you, do you miss me?' and they said yes, I would probably have said, 'Do you want to talk about things and work it out?' If he then said no, what was the point in knowing he missed me! I also recognized that asking if he missed me was quite selfish, really. It was trying to feed my own needs. What I really wanted to know was if he wanted to work things out. So why didn't I just say that?!

What I realized was I was asking for words, not actions. I also wanted to feel different or better, which was unlikely to come from interacting with The Ex. What I thought I wanted was him to tell me what I wanted to hear, but in reality, I wanted him to act differently. People can say many things that I want to hear, yet never do or act differently.

Remember, just because he loved you doesn't mean that is how you needed to be loved.

I want to clear the air

My brain would say: Ugh, wanting to clear the air is a very strong urge. I want to leave things nicely. I want to understand certain elements of the breakup, so that I won't make the same mistakes again.

What I learned to tell myself: Nope. It's just another trick of my brain. Clearing the air won't make a difference; as with previous exes, it's unlikely The Ex and I will ever talk again. It's unlikely we will be friends or share a coffee. For clearing the air to be a useful event, I'd need to be over him. Breakups create a feeling of unease in the air. Just because splitting up is unpleasant, we can only clear the air if we make up or have moved on – which they cannot help you with. You aren't making up.

The vague thought of 'I need closure' haunted me, but I wasn't even sure what I wanted closure on. I think I just wanted to stop hurting and be over him, but he couldn't give me that. Any conversation with him would give me a hit of endorphins, serotonin and oxytocin (see Chapter 1). I would feel good at that moment, but ultimately, like a drug, it would wear off and I would want more. I don't want closure, I just want to stop feeling this detox from him, and I want things to be good again. But they aren't going to be.

Once I get answers on one thing, it may open a whole box on other things. The idea of closure says I want to feel that this situation is closed off in my mind, like a treasured mystery. We worked out the issue, and now we can close that book and both move on. But even if we work out what the breaking point was, that he was in the wrong or I was, we have broken up. Working out that we were not compatible isn't exactly rocket science. I knew in my heart that this relationship wasn't working and my needs weren't being met. We have broken up for a good reason.

Once I am over him, I won't need to actively look for closure, because that chapter will have naturally closed in my mind and heart. So, in summary, I am only messaging and wanting closure because I want to talk or message him. True closure will only come when I am over him. This conversation I think I want will provide more information for my brain to mull over, for thoughts to re-evaluate, but that is not closure. It will create more questions. The feeling sad about it is mine only to deal with and get over. He can't give me that, so why message?

So these are not reasons to contact The Ex. Once I realized my brain was playing tricks on me, I ignored my brain's suggestions because I knew nothing good would come from contacting him.

I miss him

You often have this knot in your tummy as your body craves the feelings that you associate with them, and you need a hit of that feeling. I have even contacted The Ex, convincing myself that getting a shot of good feeling is a good enough reason to contact them, only to be devastated and feel strung out when he read my message but didn't reply. Fair play to him, and I later regretted it.

What I learned to tell myself: Nope. This is just your mind craving him. The impact of them replying will be short-lived. As you aren't back together, this is just a temporary fix. You will hit rock bottom if he doesn't reply.

Not being friends on social media

In the same vein, I haven't remained friends or in contact via social media with any of my exes. I believed that remaining friends would hold me back from moving on. If I couldn't answer yes to any of the questions below, I thought it best to unfriend or unfollow them:

- Did we have kids or share a pet together?
- Did we have strong mutual friends or family – i.e. are we likely to have to be around each other frequently?
- Did we work or have a business together?

If I couldn't say yes to those, I didn't try to remain friends. I wasn't saying we could never be friends, but at the key stage after a breakup, I was trying to get into a new life habit without them. Any rational person can understand that you don't feel that you can remain friends immediately after a breakup.

I think this works both ways, whether you did the breaking up or if it was mutual. Habits need to form without the other person there. Thinking habits need to be undone. Other things need to fill the space of The Ex; this can't happen if you remain friends.

Setting boundaries

If you have to remain in contact, such as working together, keep information to a minimum. Your paths may cross but avoid curiosity about what they're doing or anything additional as you settle into being apart. You want your thinking processes to create a new path without them and reducing contact or maintaining no contact for these key months is vital. If they try to share information you do not need, shut this down immediately.

Being on the receiving end of messages from The Ex

If an Ex messages me after we have broken up, I don't need to ask if he's missing me; he wouldn't have messaged me otherwise. But I would want to know why they were contacting me. Is it because their mind is missing the hit of good hormones? Are they in the habit of messaging me, or do they want to work this out?

He is doing that to make me feel bad

When you're communicating with The Ex, they can be pretty off and mean. This has happened to me no matter who did the breaking up. I believe the true judge of a person is not at the start of the relationship but how they treat you at the end. When you're hurting, you can lash out at someone with words and actions, maybe posting things on your social media either passive-aggressively aimed at The Ex 'I am living my best life now I am single' or posting photos of you with someone else.

I have always taken it as a massive compliment when my Exes have posted on Facebook things that are clearly aimed to hurt me. Because if they weren't fazed or hurting from the breakup, they wouldn't need to – because they didn't care. They wouldn't need to take a picture with someone else in public or even post anything at all if they were just enjoying time with the new person. I have friends who could almost have a flick book of men in their profile pictures, but I usually wait until things are quite certain before posting a love interest on my social media. My Exes have really hurt me when we have broken up. I have cared deeply and felt that I was slung aside as if our relationship meant nothing. I could be nasty to these Exes or react on my social media making digs, but I'd only do it because I was hurting.

Although it's a compliment in my view that Exes are posting things to try and get at me, it doesn't mean they care enough or want to rekindle the relationship. And if you're the one looking, then be aware you may see information that hurts your feelings, so that's your responsibility to avoid.

I have often had female friends say, 'He has made me feel this way,' or 'She's doing this to me,' or 'He knew the impact that would have.' No one can make you feel anything; they can trigger you, but what you feel in response is the result of your thoughts.

I believe once I've broken up with someone, how I thought and felt and for how long was on me. I am making myself feel things in their absence. The longer my thoughts linger on their life without me and whether they cared for me, the more I hurt myself in their absence. They cannot hurt me now; they are not in my life anymore. The best revenge on an Ex that has hurt you is to live the best and fullest life you can.

No one can make you feel anything. They can trigger you, but what you feel in response results from your thoughts. Truly, they can't make you feel anything.

Working stuff out with The Ex

There may come a time when you do want to contact The Ex, this has to be carefully planned and you need to ensure its not a knee jerk reaction to a sudden low mood or just a momentary lapse of judgment. You need to have been through the list above, checking all the reasons you may unnecessarily contact The Ex, such as them being a habit you need to overcome, or due to wanting answers that an Ex can never really give you. You also need to check which mood you are in (see chapter 8). Always give yourself a few days to check that this isn't a reaction in the moment.

You need to be clear and decide in your mind what it is that you want from the conversation ensuring that you are communicating as clearly as you can. By that I mean, not assuming they understand what you want and dance around the subject. You have to be prepared to accept that in the moment you contact The Ex they may not be on the same page or they may need time themselves to think things through, it could be totally out of the blue. If you are able, try and meet up somewhere you can speak honestly, long text messages or emails do not work so well.

I have gotten back with an Ex after a argument and splitting up, messaging and then meeting up to talk. I have also moved on and six months later an Ex has contacted me as if nothing had happened.

For me, what has been clear is, if they want to communicate and work things through with you, they will. If they want to be difficult they will. Just focus on being clear, if you cannot work it out, move on.

Hurtful statements that are not true

I had a friend whose Ex said she was damaged goods and would never find anyone who could take that on. That hurt her deeply, but what was worse was that she accepted it as truth. After she heard this, she would say it herself, when dates were not kind and short-term relationships failed. She would repeatedly hurt her own ego and self by repeating this to herself. It became part of her story. This was not just for weeks after the breakup, this was years later.

When I heard her refer to herself as damaged goods, I immediately asked where this had come from and was shocked that a bullying comment from a bitter Ex had left such a permanent mark. We sat for a short while picking apart this one statement, proving without a doubt that this had no evidence behind it and was not true at all. It was like a weight had been lifted off her shoulders. Her whole persona changed.

What had happened was she had decided this was true and as such it should be her reality. We looked at what she was saying to herself and in the same way that calling names at school need to be brushed off as just mean statements, comments from The Ex need to be treated the same.

Getting back together isn't always a good idea

I had a boyfriend who would ghost me from time to time. We would have great messaging and then nothing for a week or even two. When I didn't hear from him, I felt like he didn't care. If I had offended him, he should let me know, but intermittent ghosting didn't make sense. He would say he was just really busy but then I would see he was on social media at the time! I would be really elated when I finally heard from him, but this was no way to be in a relationship. The relationship rightly ended, in my view.

I have similarly had a row and split up over a guy I believed was cheating on me. He had lots of female friends. I have no reason to this day to put my finger on why being with him made me feel so insecure. It just felt – and it really was a feeling – that he was looking at other women and wasn't that into me. I have been with other boyfriends and never felt this way. We were only six months into dating, and we both had a lot on, so we only saw each other occasionally. There was something about our connection that just wasn't right. Our relationship ended because I would spend so much time feeling insecure, not believing he was where he said he was.

If you find yourself in an unhappy pattern with a partner which leads to fall outs, upsets, game playing and breakups. They may simply not be right for you. These difficulties are because something is broken, it is not working and you are not a good enough fit. You have broken up for a good reason, now you can find something better for you.

Sometimes, you just aren't right together. That's not your fault or their fault.
You can only be who you are.

In a nutshell

- If you're out with friends wanting to enjoy yourself, don't text The Ex and do not start a conversation if they message you. You cannot respond well if drunk, and it will become a major distraction and maybe ruin what could have been an amazing time.
- Your mind will try to convince you from time to time that it's a good idea to contact the Ex (e.g. wanting to be friends, ask a question, share something or get closure). You won't get the answers you think you want, so the priority is to sever these habits.
- Avoid contact and try not being friends on social media if possible; it will help you avoid learning things that might hurt you.
- Know that others cannot make you feel bad; whether their hurtful actions are on purpose or not, you decide to do that to yourself, because they are no longer in your life.

Get out your notebook

- When you have a real urge to contact The Ex, note down what you wish to contact them about and how the possible conversation would go. What is it you want to hear? What are they likely to say in real life? Do you think you will get the answer/have the interaction you want? After this exercise – do you think it's a good idea to contact them, yes or no?
- Repeat the above for anything you want to discuss with The Ex. You may find it will stop the urge to contact them at all. After all, The Ex is just a habit you're moving on from.
- If you are suffering from low confidence due to The Ex being quite mean, write a list of the mean things that The Ex has said that you feel have stayed with you. Now sit with them and seriously consider each one. Do you believe they are true? You may want to start writing out lists of evidence proving they are not. Decide that these are mean comments, like in the playground, and you will not accept them as truth. You will not feel hurt or hurt your own self based on these untruths.

If you don't love yourself, no one else can do it for you.

Chapter 6

Being Your Own Best Friend

If my best friend needed someone to cook her a healthy meal, I'd cook it. If my brother needed me to clean the house top to bottom weekly to feel good, I'd clean it. If a work colleague asked me to go for a walk at lunchtime to cheer him up, I'd go. I have done so many things for people, from family to friends to acquaintances, to help in any way I can for them to feel good and be happy.

One time my friend was home recovering from surgery. I went to her house, cleaned the downstairs for her, then cooked her and her children dinner. Another friend's dad had a serious health diagnosis. I also cooked dinner at hers and packed up the leftovers for her to eat for lunch the following day as she went from hospital visit to hospital visit. I set time aside to support a colleague through exams, giving them a couple of hours for weeks helping them practice questions and going over exam material, they passed.

I set time aside for people all the time to cheer them up or help them, but I rarely did it for myself. If I was low in mood, I'd go to bed without dinner or just eat a piece of toast. I neglected my laundry and tidying up after myself. In that way, I was being unkind to myself when I needed love the most.

I needed to be that best friend to myself that I am to others. I needed to cook healthy meals or treat myself to quality hot chocolate. I needed to make time to plan nice things for myself and not be lazy: leaving clothes on the floor and wearing dirty clothes, feeding myself the bare minimum to keep going, hiding away and self-sabotaging my work. Not just my work now, but my career that I had worked so very hard for.

I needed to be the best friend that said good things to myself when I was feeling low. I needed to protect this person who was most in need right now. This lovely body has seen me through my life to date. This lovely person who can be so lovely to others and can make such an effort to be thoughtful for others. I needed to turn all that love and energy inward. Sometimes we need to pledge allegiance to ourselves to be our own best friend. We need to promise to take care of ourselves.

So I took out my journal and started to write:

I am going to be my own best friend. So this lovely, wonderful girl can have a better day every day. Every night I am going to select clothes for her to wear the next day and make sure the makeup is tidy for her, so she knows where it all is.

- *I am a lovely person who deserves nice things to happen, and I deserve to be happy.*
- *I am beautiful, I have a beautiful soul, and I am loved by so many people.*
- *I have done nice things for people, and they remember the effort I went to.*

- *I don't deserve to beat myself up. I am a good person, and I deserve so much love.*
- *I deserve to feel happy, relaxed and settled in life.*
- *I am so lucky to have what I have and fortunate to have friends and family.*

Things I will do for her to help her be happier:

- *I will tidy her room before bed so she can wake up relaxed and settled in her surroundings.*
- *I will cook her a healthy meal (and her brother and his wife if they want any) so that she goes to bed with a full tummy and sleeps well.*
- *I will take her out for a walk at lunchtime or fetch her a treat and focus as she eats it – so she enjoys every moment of it. I will do that every day that she needs me to – because I am my own best friend.*

Loving yourself

After the breakup, I was giving myself and my brain such a hard time. I was constantly self-critical about how I had been in the relationship that had just ended. I would often swing back and forth between feeling like this breakup was the best thing that had ever happened and that we should have done it sooner, to criticizing the days I wasn't the best I could have been with The Ex and saving this relationship.

I was spending a lot of time thinking things like:

- Why can't you be as clever as that girl?
- Why can't you dress as cool as her?
- Why aren't you in shape?

- You aren't funny like that girl.
- You're working hard on this, but that girl has achieved more, and she's younger.
- People just don't like you.
- You're hard to love because you're so annoying.
- You aren't very pretty.
- You aren't very interesting.
- You aren't special.

I was so mean to myself most of the time. Whenever I saw a pretty woman on TV, in the pub or walking past, I compared myself to her, even though I looked good. I had lost weight, I was more active, and had spent more time buying new clothes and throwing out some old ones (mostly the ones The Ex had always pulled a bit of a face at despite them being perfectly good clothes).

One day, it occurred to me that if I really don't like myself and if I believe that everyone else has so much to offer compared to me, how can anyone else love me? If I didn't love myself, would I let anyone else love me? Would I try and convince them that I wasn't a good catch because I couldn't see my own worth, which would inevitably sabotage the relationship? Whose job is it to love me? If I couldn't see my value, would I believe them or distrust them when they say they love me? I kept reading quotations and the following two really stuck out:

'Today you are You, that is truer than true.
There is no one alive who is Youer than You.'
DR SEUSS

'You are you, and that is your superpower.'
UNKNOWN

And that's true. My brain always counteracted 'you are unique and special' with 'just like everyone else'. Wow, I always had a way to belittle myself. If this rings true for you too, it's vital to address this and ask yourself, 'Whose job is it to love me?'

Yes, my mum loved me, but that was different. But why was it such a distant and abstract thought that I should love myself? I saw people putting themselves first all the time, but I never did. From then on, I decided it was my job to look out for my best interests, to care for myself. It was no one else's job to do that for me. Only I could do that for myself. I needed to put myself first and care for myself first. Like in an aeroplane safety video, I needed to put my own oxygen mask on before thinking of anyone else's.

When you don't ever put yourself first, it teaches others to put you second. They learn that you act like that, so they treat you accordingly.

What does loving yourself look like?

I started to wonder what loving myself would look like. I was driving when this thought had popped into my head, and I started to digest it. What if, instead of comparing myself negatively to others, I looked at myself as if I was the most unique and wonderful person in the world? What if I imagined that I was the perfectly imperfect main character in a romantic movie? The girl has quirks like she needs three sugars in her coffee or she always has to skip the third step on the library stairs. She always dresses as if she's out of a summer fashion website and wears a specific jewellery item from a late grandma, and has some hilarious stories, such as when she once tried to save a cat and fell out of a tree. Those types of films.

Ask yourself: If I am the lead in that romantic movie, if I am the unique and beautiful lead of my own film – then how much can I love myself?

All these films in which the key character was put on a pedestal had nothing I didn't. I can be the main character in my own love story.

In the film, she skipped the third step at the library.

Me: There is a slab on the pavement by work which, in my mind, is the wrong way round. I posted it on my social media and mentioned it at work as it frustrated me so much. I had colleagues agreeing with me, and others specifically went out to see it. There were jokes in the office to see if we could write a letter to the council to turn it around or have a group in the middle of the night just come out and correct it.

Film lead = 0 Me, the main character in my life = 1

Think about what makes you unique, then gather up as much self-love as you can muster – then note it down in your journal. Even think about what your best friends would say about you if they were writing your eulogy. What would people closest to you think about you? Here's what I observed about myself:

- I brought my handbag on a day trip to Leeds to meet a friend. On the train, I realized it had a hole in the side which I likely lost things through. My friend was late, as always, so I went into a shop, found the perfect bag and binned the old one right there outside the shop. I remember it felt amazing.
- I have two good-sized circle scars on the back of my hand, from when I rode my brother's bike into a brick wall and lost the flesh

of my knuckles as I almost went over the handlebars. I couldn't reach the brakes and pedals when the bike was so big.

- My eyes are off brown – not quite brown, not quite grey. No one has ever said I have pretty eyes, but I love their colour when I put on my makeup and mascara.
- I get really stressed when I am late for things. I get in a right flap. When I arrive, I apologize profusely, so they know I care. Other people can be late and act as if it never happened. I always apologize. Once I'm seated on a plane on time, I always say out loud, 'Ahh, made it.'
- I love to save snails that are stranded on the pavement. I will never just walk by for them to be crushed by another walker; I will always stop and transfer them to a safe bit of grass. I've taken at least three wood pigeons to wildlife sanctuaries. Then I feel guilty that I do not contribute to these sanctuaries other than bringing them birds, so I give them a good donation.
- In a previous job, I'd always decorated my colleagues' desks on their birthdays to make them smile.
- I eat the toffee layer of a Twix first, then the biscuit.
- I set up a staircase challenge at work to get the team away from the desks during a restructure when everyone was a little depressed.
- One time I forgot a discount voucher for £6 off a shop and was low on money, so I cried – then crashed my car due to the tears. I wanted to hug myself after recalling this memory.
- There's a wisp of baby hair at the top right of my face. I hate it, but it's a hilarious personal battle and a daily challenge. I should name that wisp, then we can be proper friends.

- I love walking in the rain with my raincoat on and do not care about getting soaked.

So I started to reframe the negative things I was saying to myself. Relabelling things about me. Thinking of things I criticized about myself and changing them to think of them as things I struggle with but that I will lovingly support myself about

- I love the way you care. You care about people so much. You try too hard and then get so upset at yourself. You don't have to do all these things to feel something or impress others.
- I love that you get so tense about things. I wish you would relax more and just let the world exist, let it float there and not affect you.
- I love you. I love you for all the things you are. The things you find funny, the things you find sad, the things that scare you, the things you don't like.
- I love that you worry about how you present yourself, you always feel like such a klutz, but I'm sure you're more admired than you know.
- I love that you think you aren't that pretty when beauty isn't measured by one specific look. You're wonderful to look at and be around, which makes you, you.
- I love how you always feel a little awkward with silences, and so you're really good at making the first move to talk to others, and others have said how welcoming you are.
- I love how you overthink old events and beat yourself up as if you can be perfect at all times when those imperfections have created great connections with others.

After doing this journaling exercise, I started to really feel love from myself through the eyes of someone who loves me and finds me so special. I felt a warm glow as if I was special, beautiful, and admired, and it only took 10 minutes or so initially thinking about it in the car and then writing down my thoughts. I hope you'll feel this glow too, when you do this for yourself.

One day, this life will be over. Don't waste time not seeing your own potential in every moment. Your body has carried you and taken care of you, so take time to love it. Remember that your thoughts protect you and keep you safe, so love them and be your own best friend.

I used to think that I was tired of being me. Everywhere I went, there I was! I couldn't run away from myself. I could change my circumstances, but everything I was went with me into this new change. In my head, I would say things like, *I hate my life, I hate who I am.*

I had no reason to hate myself this much. I was my own worst enemy and needed to learn to be my own best friend. There was the me interacting with others, the ego me that had opinions on things, the me that consciously made decisions. Then I felt there was the authentic me, or 'her' as I call it. My soul, my body, my spirit. The conscious me can hear bad news and come out with a comment appropriate to the moment, while the 'her' that is my soul, body and spirit doesn't have words – the heartbreak and agony are palpable. She has emotions such as pain and joy but never words. When I have sobbed myself to sleep alone, this person is there with me. It's the part of me that cries suddenly when I see another in pain. The knot in the throat. She is with me, and she hurts.

I've taken this soul, body and spirit for granted and I've loved her for how amazing she was. She has had battles and bad times, and she has had her good times, when her hard work has come to fruition. I haven't congratulated her enough for her successes. I haven't sat back and said, 'Well done!' I've called her fat. I've belittled her using my internal voice, telling her others are better than her. I've removed her confidence by telling her that she's not funny when she really is. I've kicked her when she was down by telling her she was ugly when she's beautiful – when she's just herself. I've fed her chocolate to make her feel better and then told her she's a disgusting fat pig. Through all of this, it's me and her.

I saw how she had tried to carry me when I was down, carried me through her hard times, but I was also the source of those hard times. I decided to love her and be a better friend going forward. But I do love the person I am. Now I love every little bit of this body I get to go through this life with.

Making pleasurable moments

To ensure I remembered that every day is a gift and to be enjoyed, I needed to think of one thing that would make me happy. This needed to be my first thought of the day when I was in the shower and getting dressed.

What can you do today to make yourself happy?

I set myself the task of doing something pleasurable for myself every day. It could be anything from drinking a Bailey's hot chocolate, setting up a call with a friend, going for a walk at lunchtime or having one of the monster slices of cake from the canteen to meditating for 20 minutes before bed, visualizing the future and focusing on soothing my unconscious mind – to help with the 3 a.m. awakenings. I deserved this pleasurable moment in each day and decided I would do this for myself as I would do for a friend without hesitation.

Sometimes I would tell myself there is no time to do it now, or I should really think about the calories, or I am too tired to make myself a special healthy dinner and would just have toast. I would argue with myself in my mind, saying, 'This is what your soul self wanted and needed this morning. What she wants to feel better, we will do together, no compromises.'

For example, I might tell myself, 'Today I will get a hot chocolate from the cafe around the corner with Baileys. I won't gulp it down unconsciously while checking my phone or reading an article on my computer. I'll take time to smell, hear and see the colours, scents and sounds around me and mindfully enjoy the whole thing. I can't keep washing away these moments of joy by flicking between things. I need to have pleasurable moments every day and remember life is wonderful.

I also wrote in my journal all the nice daily things I was doing to remind myself of the wonderful things I had done for myself.

In a nutshell

- We take time to be kind to others but often don't extend the same patience, tolerance, love and support to ourselves.
- Start by loving yourself. Understanding all the little things about yourself that make you, you.
- Look at yourself through the eyes of your best friend, remembering the great things you've done, the things you've done for others and the joy you have brought them.
- Your soul, body and spirit have been with you through all of your hardest and lowest times; take care of them and love them.
- Start each day by asking yourself what one thing you could do for yourself that day to make yourself happy and do it without compromise.
- Really enjoy that moment, and make sure you practise self-care and self-love every day.

Get out your notebook

- If your best friend was looking at you and writing about you, what would they write about you? What nice stories do they have?
- Write in a romantic movie style, where you're the main character. Focus especially on things the movie would highlight such as your lovely features, things that make you unique and different, your little habits and quirks.
- Then list great things that you have done and experienced.
- Write down one thing every day that would make your day better and make sure you do it for yourself. Document what you completed for yourself in a diary or daily planner.

'Just because drama knocks, you don't have to open the door.'

—Anon

Chapter 7

Avoiding Derailing, Triggers and Bombshells

My days were now disciplined. I got up and showered first, dressed in clothes that made me feel confident and good. I didn't need to think about it in the morning because I laid out my outfit the night before. Plus, if there was a particular outfit I wanted to feel good in, I'd wash it and hang it up the night before, so it was dry for me in the morning.

I thought about something that would bring me joy. To start, I bought a really nice granola cereal with nuts and fruit. I really enjoyed eating that in the morning, which fuelled my body with energy. Sometimes I even made my ham and salad sandwiches the night before, so I didn't need to worry about lunch.

I listened to Calvin Harris or other dance music from the 1980s or 2000s blasting out the car. I sat up straight, took mindful breaks, said nice things to myself, looked at positive messages from friends. I also talked to people during the day and focused on my work. When I got home, I sorted my clothes for the next day, laundered my clothes or hung them up, and tidied my room before bed. Before long, I was sleeping until 6 a.m. without any interruptions.

I knew there would be setbacks. I knew if I was going to start to feel better, I needed to stop all the things that made me feel bad or brought on the negative emotions which could derail my happiness. Keeping my brain calm wasn't easy. I had accepted that The Ex was going to be in my brain and that my brain would naturally search for ways to think about The Ex, and that was a natural and comfortable path for my brain. But I wanted to be aware of the triggers to avoid.

Other people derailing you

So, I was doing well. I was doing the right things, and I was no longer self-sabotaging myself. I felt good. Even though I was eating more, I was losing weight from moving my body more in the day and getting out to see friends.

However, when it comes to staying on the path to having a good day, you can't just plan on yourself as external factors can derail your day too. I needed to plan for those. So I started to list the things that had derailed me in the recent past, on days that didn't go well, in order to identify the root cause so that I could avoid those days in future.

Sweeping statement bombs

The first one is what I will nickname the sweeping statement bomb. This bomb is generally set off by acquaintances but can be done by friends who aren't thinking. So what is it?

There was a secretary who worked in my office. Middle-aged, always going on about breaking her diet but with no signs of actually being on one. She was collecting for a raffle but being rather slow about it. I was doing well, looking good. I was focusing hard and ploughing through a piece of work. I felt very productive and happy. She sauntered over to my desk, saying, 'Hey lovely, do you want to contribute to the raffle?' While I was looking for a £1 coin to buy a ticket, she asked me how I was doing, but in a very sad tone while giving me this look where she tilted her head, stuck out her bottom lip, then drew it in whilst shrugging her shoulders. The whole combination of movements drew my attention to the fact that she was asking about my private life.

I said I was fine, and she went on to ask if I'd heard from The Ex. When I replied that I hadn't, she said, 'I wonder why he hasn't been in contact. Do you think it has been over a while for him?' I said, 'I don't know.' She shrugged her shoulders, exchanged my money for tickets, then said 'Strange' and walked off to the next desk.

There it was – a 'sweeping statement bomb' – sat in my lap. Three – two – one – and my brain exploded with confusion at the statement.

I turned to my computer, thinking, 'Right, back to work.' However, my motivation was gone. My head was in a whirl. I was now sitting with my fingers poised over the computer keys but not looking at the screen. *What did she mean by 'over a while'? Am I intolerable? What did she mean? Can she tell a guy would have had enough of me? It's not like I can ask her what she meant, even if she hadn't just left the office.* My brain is dull, and I'm confused, hurt and.... well, I just feel like crap. In that small interchange, I'd gone from coping to crashing. What the heck had just happened?

Another time in the kitchen, as I walked in to make my cup of tea, a colleague asked me how I was doing and if I was still at my brother's house. I said that I was taking every day as it came and that it wasn't ideal, but I was fortunate to have somewhere to go. She pried a little further, asking if I had heard from the Ex, I said no and was ready to leave it there. I added coffee to my mug; at this point, she has finished making her tea, but there is apparently too much silence for her, and she filled the silent gap, and inadvertently ruined my day, my ability to eat dinner and possibly even my ability to sleep that night by dropping a sweeping statement bomb: 'Do you think he met someone else?' It was just an offhand comment, but in my head, I screamed, *'No, I didn't think that... but I do now!'* This sweeping statement left me a dithering mess.

In both of these instances, as far as the other person was concerned, they were just making small talk. They probably wouldn't want me to think The Ex had moved on or that he was cheating. They were just making a comment.

I was always angry when I got derailed, but this is the essence of small talk. When there's a silence, people fill it with meaningless conversation. These small exchanges keep things civil. When you know a little information about someone, you return to that information repeatedly. You don't overthink it; you don't want to have too long of a conversation, you aren't invested in the conversation and therefore don't really put much thought into it.

A great example is a guy in our team who played the guitar, and by playing the guitar, I mean he mentioned once that he had been given an old guitar and thought he might learn a bit about it. That tiny titbit was shared in a 'been up to anything nice' conversation in front of a few of us, and following this one interaction, the team manager would always ask about the guitar playing, to which the team member would just say, 'Good, still trying.' It didn't change, he didn't appear to play anymore, and the team manager never seemed to find a new opener to ask the team member about. He even mentioned that he hadn't bothered to touch the guitar in months, but people kept asking.

I knew I had to look at these questions about The Ex or the breakup in a similar light and not treat them as genuine questions but silence fillers. People have two minutes away from their computer, they don't want to think too hard about it. Commenting on the pieces of my life are one step up from what is on television, the weather at the weekend, have you turned your heating on yet, the first lawn mow of the season and where to go on holiday. These coworkers are therefore not going to give me advice on my relationship that is thought-out and meaningful, and nor should they really.

People need something to talk about. In the absence of anything else, we might ask about the weather, health, or parents and children, so don't let meaningless small talk derail your best efforts.

Emotional grenades

This can happen with friends and acquaintances too. You may find from time to time that a friend will text to ask, 'How are you doing?' followed by 'Have you heard from him?'

These emotional grenades also derailed me. I would be sitting there happily going about my day, then receive this message from a friend and take it as an opportunity to share something I had been thinking about that week and feedback on how I had been feeling. Sometimes, there was something that I was thinking about or something I had been struggling with, and I was relieved to get another person's opinion.

However, this 'how are you' query may also be them making small talk. Sometimes it's a text version of small talk when they have two minutes waiting for a bus, for an order to be delivered, in-between their programme starting or a date arriving. They wanted to check in but were not planning on opening Pandora's box.

I didn't realize this and generally would share some vulnerable information. Consequently, I would get a brush-off one-liner response, 'Ah, never mind,' or no response, then 'Sorry, I was off out.' They were just killing time on their end and hadn't planned on getting into a long conversation.

I was going about my day perfectly fine, until their message invited me to share something I didn't need to, which encouraged me to think about things I didn't want to. But once I'd shared something personal, there was this wait for a response, I was sat, feeling as if I were holding open a wound. Feeling exposed, a little offended, a little angry at them and myself. I felt rejected and not interesting. These exchanges kept me stuck in a negative cycle of thought. My friend texted me, dropped in the emotional grenade and let it go off.

If a friend texts to ask about the breakup, they don't want long paragraphs. As these are silence fillers over text, you don't want to open yourself up to a moment where they can cast a generalized statement. This will leave you with an emotional grenade, where their advice keeps you awake for a week as it's given your brain extra information to overanalyse. They are just checking in, just seeing how you are, not preparing to answer your uttermost difficult internal questions. If you were hanging out together for a few hours, you can go into more detail, but don't allow yourself to be derailed by this kind of text. Accept this is simply an 'I'm checking in on you' text. Not 'I'm here to save you from your own pattern of thinking' text.

I decided that I didn't want to share information anymore about the breakup with others. It gave them something interesting to talk about, but I would be left feeling emotionally exhausted and hurt. I wished

I hadn't even mentioned the breakup to some people, as there was no reason to make my breakup the centrepiece of things to talk about.

I also found that some friends were drawn to talk about it when I really didn't want to. And so, it was best to only share information about the breakup with my tight circle of friends to prevent myself from being derailed and only to discuss it when we were in person, and I knew I had their attention.

In later breakups, I would decide I needed to control the information I shared to prevent this vulnerable feeling that people knew too much about me and sometimes acted as if I was a little broken. I shouldn't have let myself indulge in this level of sharing as it had created this situation whereby others asked about my private life to make small talk.

The subject of your painful, heart-wrenching breakup should not be the topic of idle chitchat, so share your innermost feelings only with those you trust and choose the right time to do it.

However, it was too late now, people knew, so what could I do to avoid the sweeping statement bomb? What can I do now to avoid the emotional grenade that was the generic questioning small talk about your relationship? I came up with the method I nicknamed the three-line diversion.

The three-line diversion

After testing, I found that those prone to dropping sweeping statement bombs or emotional grenades only asked about my relationship three times.

Potential sweeping statement bombs always start off quite innocent – 'How are you?' or 'Hey you, how have you been?' That's easy enough. The worst one, the most disarming, is the 'Are you OK?' with the overly sympathetic tone and look.

To win at these interactions, you need to own them and hop over them like the Road Runner getting away from Wile E. Coyote. Here is how I learned to roll with them:

'Hey, good, thanks,' I say. 'You?'

'Yeah, good, how are things going at your new place?' They bat back, not going into any detail about their own life.

Now, before I became wise, at this stage, I may have automatically started to answer the bombardment of questions, 'Yes, settled in the new house, I really like it.'

The next questions are more probing questions like:

- 'Have you met anyone yet?' If you say no, it will always be closely followed by 'Don't worry – you have time.'
- 'Are you going to stay there? What's your plan?'
- 'Have you spoken to or seen The Ex?'

This can trap you into sharing information that can make you feel vulnerable because you know your situation may not be what you wanted. It appeared their interest was superficial, but now they specifically asked you a question on the subject they were referring to, looking for a little juicy gossip. The importance here was that the second question was around the relationship or what you're doing. Now the questions are prying around things that are quite emotive. This could open you up to the sweeping statement bomb – where the conversation ends on a statement from them that hurts your feelings.

This needs to be closed down. This is where you need to keep strong. You can't come out with something cliché with no detail as there is nothing they can latch onto. They want to get more information.

It is good to share something you're doing to change the subject and daintily manoeuvre away from the suspect sweeping statement bomber. They have to be statements that shut down the conversation, divert it elsewhere and leave you feeling empowered. But most importantly, you must remove the opportunity for them to leave you an emotional wreck.

After some trialling and testing, I came up with three strong lines.

Sweeping statement bomber: 'How have you been?'

Reply: 'I have been great, thanks. I have written a list of challenges I want to do before the end of the year. Keep it interesting. Do you have any big plans this year?' (Note here typical sweeping statement bomber will ignore the interesting bits in your life and ask about the relationship again.)

Sweeping statement bomber: 'How are things with The Ex? Heard from him?' or 'How are things at your new home?' Or: 'Met anyone new yet?'

This next response must have a deflection comment, to change the subject.

Reply: 'I have been mostly focusing on my training for a half-marathon lately, to be honest. Have you ever done one?' Or: 'I have been mostly focusing on my exams lately, to be honest. Do you have any courses you're doing this year?' Or: 'I have been focusing on my charity event lately. Do you have any things you're doing this year?' Or: 'I have been mostly focusing on booking a holiday lately. Do you have any holidays booked this year?'

This is where the sweeping statement bomber has tried to pry, but because you haven't actually told them anything they don't appear to have anything further. They thought they would get some juicy gossip and have come away empty-handed.

Sometimes if people don't give up after a second question, they will try a third time. They can also be more direct this time. So you need an exit strategy if you're stuck in a space with them, or another deflector if the conversation is happening over text. The exit strategy is where you ask them a defined question that has a defined end.

Sweeping statement bomber: 'So, how are you finding things on your own?' Or 'I'm guessing you haven't heard from The Ex.'

Reply: 'Oh gosh, life is nonstop right now, isn't it? But I was looking at new jewellery lately and wondered where you got your necklace from?' (Even if the necklace is hideous.) 'I've got to go.'

This way, you haven't made it look like you're being defensive or don't want to talk, as that may make them want to question you more.

Other exit strategies are anything to get their opinion which is usually effective to change the subject. For example:

- I want to book a holiday with the girls. Where do you think I should go?
- I think I might change my car; what do you think I should have?
- I think a weekend break will be good for me, any ideas where to go?

The three-line diversion was helpful when people asked how I was in passing. Also, I chose to use this when friends texted me, or if I was having a really good time with friends and didn't want to talk about The Ex. Because good friends are going to enquire about it because they care about you, but also because it's a topic to talk about.

I found it key to work out when was a good time to share my concerns or negative feelings on the situation and when to deploy the three-line diversion. I'd ruined a few nice afternoons discussing what happened between The Ex and me; as described in Chapter 1, my brain was used to thinking of him and entered into these discussions to discover new information about him. To get out of the habit of him, I needed to stop talking about him. Not only that, but I felt boring, selfish and self-involved. Even though I didn't always bring it up, my friends often encouraged the conversation in that direction. Sometimes the best part of a two-hour meet-up was about me, The Ex and theories as to why it ended and what he's doing now. So I chose to use the three-line diversion with friends and acquaintances as I only wanted to think positively about the breakup.

Friends want to ask, but don't let it derail you. If you talk about The Ex, remind yourself to use an exit strategy statement if the conversation goes on for too long to keep your time with your friends positive and fun.

Removing triggers

Sometimes when looking through my phone messages or emails for something, an old email or message chain from The Ex would pop up. I would read it and be taken back to that moment, and it would start a domino effect of thinking that I didn't need to go through. I could do my best to just ignore those old messages and keep them, but ultimately the best thing was to delete them all. I decided to keep the photos but archive them somewhere, but whatever was said when we were together didn't exist now. I knew plucking out any specific messages I wanted to keep would depress me.

I'd previously kept emails from other Exes and knew I would never read them again and I knew it would be the same this time. I selected The

Ex's name and number on my phone. Select and delete all. Some people keep messages on their phones, but I knew that looking through them would make me sad. There were also emails on my work email address. I knew it wasn't constructive to read them at work, so I deleted them. I knew I couldn't read these texts or emails again in this headspace. On the slim possibility that we talked again and worked things out, what had gone before wouldn't help me. I had to start fresh. So there was no need to keep them; it would do nothing but bring me down and derail me. If my best friend had split from her partner, I wouldn't keep showing her messages from her Ex. This isn't productive to a workday. Even if I read them in my break, I wouldn't be as productive or in the right mindset.

Delete or archive old messages and texts. Reading them again will only bring up memories that won't serve you in moving forward.

In Chapter 4, we covered how changing your routine breaks the habit of being with The Ex, but some non-daily triggers are also helpful to avoid. For example, as well as changing my perfume and soundtrack, I also changed what I ordered at the takeaway. I didn't want to trigger any old thoughts or memories. The Ex and I always ordered the same chicken tikka masala and garlic naan for him, mushroom balti and Peshwari naan for me. We had so many discussions around the naan we chose over the years. He didn't like mine; I didn't like his, although from time to time, we would do a taste test swap that always ended in 'I prefer mine.' I decided that I would order something new, and if it was good, I wouldn't order the other dish for some time.

In a nutshell

- When you're getting on the right track after a breakup, it's not just your own mindset you need to focus on. You can be derailed by people around you. So get ready to avoid sweeping statement bombs and emotional grenades.
- If you need to talk things through about The Ex, choose who and when you want this to happen. This will prevent lengthy discussions about The Ex from spoiling fun plans with friends and leaving you feeling down.
- Choose the people and times for which you'll need a three-line diversion to deal with a sweeping statement bomb or emotional grenade to divert yourself away from questioning and avoid leaving yourself vulnerable.
- You may also wish to remove other triggers like old emails from The Ex on your computer – at home and work – and old messages on your phone.
- If you had habits with The Ex like eating the same foods or going to the same place, make these exciting by choosing something new and different from the menu or eating somewhere totally new.

Get out your notebook

- Write down a few people at work, acquaintances and even friends who are likely to ask about your relationship in a superficial way, making small talk or sending a short text message which has previously or could possibly derail you.
- Write down several statements that could be useful as lines of diversion. Think about things that you're interested in right now, things that you could talk enthusiastically about and easily.
- Look at the list of people and link these with lines of diversion you could use on them. Play this in your mind before you see them. At the end of this exercise, you should have at least three strong diversion answers to try out.
- Think of any other triggers in your day that may have derailed you recently. Think through how these can be avoided in your routine.

Whether you think you can get over them, or you think you can't – you're right.[10]

[10] Based on the original quote by Henry Ford: 'Whether you think you can or you think you can't, you're right!'

Chapter 8

What You Think Is What You Feel

Henry Ford said, 'Whether you think you can, or you think you can't, you're right.' In the same way, whatever you believe you going through, you're right. This is so true when you're recovering from heartbreak... but what do I mean?

This quote applies to every element of your day and life, and it is important to focus on what your thoughts are telling you. There are days when you might think, 'I cannot cope with this heartbreak. I am not lovable. I will never meet someone. The Ex will meet someone first. I am ugly. I don't have [*enter any quality you feel you lack*]. I am [*enter any quality you hate about yourself*].' But when you focus and control your thoughts better, your thoughts can help you feel like a winner instead of a loser.

Some people have been victims of crimes, experienced horrific ordeals and yet appear to come out the other side unscathed. As in, they keep going. They don't give up on themselves. Some have had a comfortable life but constantly complain about minor problems or challenges. They never have a positive word to say and talk as if the world is against them. Some people live with disabilities and show remarkable resilience in not letting it stand in their way. Others don't turn up for themselves if they wake up late or don't have a specific outfit. Your mindset and how you talk to yourself after the breakup will massively impact how you move on from it.

Those that see a breakup as an impossible situation to feel good about will feel that way. Those that see a breakup as something sad but possible to move on from will feel that way. What you think is what you feel.

Comedy or drama frame of mind

Let's look at how your day can go. You can see it as a comedy or a drama. You can have the mindset of someone who will never get over The Ex or someone who thinks, 'Oh well, onwards and upwards.' The emotions you feel are not a choice, but the thoughts which drive how you feel are. You can decide never to get over The Ex, look a mess, think sad thoughts all day and be miserable. Or you can decide to think positively about the situation and remind yourself of all the opportunities coming your way.

When faced with difficult times, choosing to think positively about it made me feel so much happier, and I realized I could choose to live a drama or a comedy. Let's look at how each choice plays out in the real world.

Living the drama

A girl walks into a pub on a sunny day. All that runs through her mind is her recent breakup, how unfair it was, that she will never meet anyone like her Ex. Her clothes aren't ironed. In fact, they are barely clean because she couldn't pull herself together enough to work out what she was going to wear to meet her friend. She didn't shower. Her hair is a mess. She walks into the pub feeling and looking dishevelled. She slumps down next to her best friend and removes her sunglasses, revealing puffy eyes and two-day-old eyeliner. She talks depressingly, revealing that she feels there is little point or meaning to moving around and engaging in daily activities. Her friend consoles her. That's what friends do. The friend doesn't need to ask about The Ex as the conversation is driven by the topic. Her friend reminds her that it will all be OK. Despite these reassurances, when the girl notices a cute guy in the corner, she thinks: *What is he looking at? He probably thinks I'm a mess and what a waste of space. That's how I feel.* The girl cries a little. *What's the point in hiding it?* The friends remain for an hour and then leave. The girl slumps home.

When I was stuck in the drama mentality, I was the loser in the situation. I succumbed to the pain and decided that it was a certainty, that this did and should hurt. The Ex didn't want me anymore, and as a result, I wasn't datable. Or at least I wouldn't find anyone like The Ex. Many good things could be happening around me, but they were around me, and I didn't connect with them. I focused on the problems around me and how I would fail. There were new people I could have met, new opportunities I could have taken up, but my thinking was drama. My world was miserable and empty.

Living the comedy

A girl walks into a pub on a sunny day. All that runs through her mind are her plans for the day and this week, how she needs to get out there to meet new people and make new friends. She is wearing an old dress that makes her look amazing – sometimes oldies are goodies. She had rushed to get ready as she was out late with friends last night. She looks at herself in the mirror next to the pub door, straightens her hair, and tidies her eyeliner. She takes a seat next to her best friend removes the sunglasses she knows make her look good (they only cost £6.99, but no one else knows). She jokes, 'Who wouldn't want this?' and gestures to herself as she smiles at her friend. She talks positively and animatedly because she is a good friend, bringing out the best in her. Her conversation is driven by what she will do this year, photos of recent nights out and discussions of the funny book she's recently finished. Her friend makes some great recommendations of new restaurants to try and great walks they can go on. The friend asks for details on the relationship – 'Have you heard from him?' She deploys the three-step sweeping statement bomb diversion (see Chapter 7); she's not being side-tracked into negativity today. In the mix of it all, she notices a very cute guy in the corner of the pub. Her friend reminds her that it will all be OK and gives her pointers on places to meet people, people she can probably go out with. They laugh together. They remain for an hour and then leave. The girl goes home with more new plans.

On my good days, the comedy days, I was the winner in any situation I was in and felt amazing, fun and unique. I thought about how I had a lot to offer, and how much The Ex would miss my spontaneity and humour. I would see all the good things happening around me, and I enjoyed being with good-spirited people. I was invited to numerous events and weekends away. I took up new opportunities and met new people. I was thinking comedy, and my world was happy and abundant.

You choose your mindset

What is the difference between comedy and drama? The mentality. What you CHOOSE to focus on.

I could tell from how I held my body when I didn't want to look after myself and my good habits slid. I wasn't setting up situations to get the best from them. In an effort to get back to a better mindset, I would remind myself of the positive outcomes of disciplining myself and choosing to do the things that would keep my mind positive and in the comedy mentality.

The funny thing is when I was in a good mood and had positive energy – good things would happen. Like, I'd make a new friend, or suddenly get a text about someone who had a ticket to an event. The feelings would spiral upwards, and good things were drawn to the happy energy I was giving off.

When my mood was bad, negative things appeared to be drawn to me. I'd tread in dog muck because I was lost in my head. Distracted, I wouldn't follow conversations and miss out on things. I'd be cut up by other drivers or have someone be rude to me in a shop. These things seemed to happen more when I felt rotten; it was a downward spiral of negative energy.

Did you know that energy can attract similar energy, or maybe you get more of what you focus on? Either way, the more I kept my mind in a moody, self-defeating depressed state, the more reasons I had to stay that way, the more things around me became negative and not nice. The days I was happy and positive, I found more reasons and opportunities to be happy. The days went well and I had more reasons to be positive.

Sometimes the decision to have a good day starts as soon as you wake up. Other times you'll need to kick yourself into doing something nice for yourself, having some time to feel grateful, going for a walk and quiet time to change your energy.

Facing a setback and dealing with panic

At some point, you'll have to prepare for something negative to happen, or you'll hear or see something which may cause you to feel great pain from the breakup and a spiral of other thoughts and feelings all at once. Examples may be bumping into The Ex, them texting you, trawling their social media to see them super happy or with someone else, noticing their relationship status changing, a date standing you up, encountering a troll on a dating app or a guy you quite like messaging then totally ghosting you. Unfortunately, I wasn't ready for the setback when it happened, and it hurt.

I noticed this guy on a dating app. I really liked his profile and pictures, so I messaged him. I sent a short three-line message mentioning what I liked about his profile, and said it would be nice to hear from him. The guy messaged back two words: 'Jog on.' I was so shocked by his response I had to Google to confirm it was as horrid as I thought. *Go away; get lost; beat it. Primarily heard in the UK.* Unfortunately not linked to the activity between walking and running in this instance.

I kept telling myself this was just a troll, but his message somehow hurt my feelings. Perhaps I was low on sleep that day, a little stressed or hormonal, but it started a whole chain reaction of thoughts and actions that I decided I wanted to avoid in future. So I tried to unravel what led to the event, like recounting the individual steps of scientists before the fire, air and fuel came together in an explosion. I wanted to understand in myself what happened next to unpick it.

I sat back and thought, what's the point. I told myself it was just a stupid troll. But that quickly escalated to telling myself I couldn't do this. I don't want to do this anymore. I don't want to be on dating sites. And then: 'I'm never going to meet anyone. How long do I have to do this for? How long do I have to put myself out there?' I felt like an air grenade had gone off, I felt shaky, sick, and unable to hear due to my ears ringing. My train had left the tracks, and it was careering towards a tree, and God knows what else following that.

My thoughts didn't stop there. My brain started to list everything I hated about my life at that moment: 'I don't want to go to work and be like this in front of others. I hate my job. I hate my life. Everything in my life is broken. Maybe I should start new elsewhere. Maybe I should move to another city or country and start again. How is it I am living with my brother? What a loser I am. Single, hate my job and nowhere to live to call my own, no real savings, nothing going for me.'

I had this panic rise up in me, that I needed to do something, that I needed to start looking for a new house and a new job, that everything was broken, that nothing was going right. Where should or could I even start? How long would it take to get out of this? I'm single, living with my brother and doing a job I am no good at. How had my life gone so wrong in the last few months? From happy in my job, with a boyfriend in a house we shared, to this. I have nothing.

I was panicked and unsettled. I felt nauseous and didn't want to eat. I felt like all of my uncertainties needed to be solved and fixed. Like something bad would happen, or I had been attacked and needed to work out what the hell just happened… hello head spin.

At these times, when you feel vulnerable and surrounded by flux, it helps to have a coping mechanism for avoiding being derailed, but what can help?

No action – sit in the moment

I realized that the scared nature of my thoughts was putting my brain into some form of survival mode. My body felt like it was firing off adrenaline, ready for an attack – as if my thoughts had somehow kicked my fight or flight response. I felt panicked. What was happening to me? I wanted to focus on how I had moved from waking up this morning to being in bits and needing to sort my life out now. All because of that one message. That one troll message. What was the urgency? I realized that nothing in my life had changed from before the message to after. I was living in the same house. Doing the same job. Nothing had changed other than receiving a mean message from a dating site troll. It had made me feel insulted, vulnerable and dissatisfied with my life situation. This one incident had derailed me.

It suddenly dawned on me in the panic that the decisions that I had to make in the coming weeks and months – didn't need to happen today. I didn't need to move house today, get a new job today, nothing needed to happen today. These thoughts helped my body to start to feel physically calmer.

When you feel panicked by thoughts about the future, remember, nothing needs to happen now, but taking good care of yourself. Repeat it like a mantra: 'Nothing needs to happen now but taking good care of myself.'

I started to observe my body in response to these scary thoughts, and I talked to myself in a best friend way. *Look at how your hand is shaking. You really stirred yourself up then, didn't you? You will be OK.* By taking control of my own thoughts and changing my own internal voice to sound like my best friend talking to me, I could come back into the moment. *All these things you're worried about will come in time.* I could see the scary thoughts more clearly, and decided I could have them, but I didn't need to do anything. I can worry about my home, my job and my single status. I can see those worries, but I don't have to act on them and panic. It will all come in time.

I needed to watch these panicked thoughts as if they were traffic or birds flying around in my head. But I didn't need to catch them or stop them. I could just watch them, knowing I didn't need to do anything about them now. These decisions would all come in time. I then learned to refocus on the moment by asking: 'What is the best thing for me to focus on today?'

The answer was usually along the lines of defining small jobs that I could complete that day. For example, 'I will work for the day and go home and take care of myself, by cooking myself a meal, laying out my clothes and getting some sleep.'

To get out of a head spin and come back to the moment, try writing down three jobs that you need to do and any tasks that need to be done around them to progress the work. Whenever you feel distracted, panicked or zoned out, look back at this paper and focus on these three jobs.

Recognising that I was in panic mode and just needed to focus on small jobs helped me get through the day and get home feeling OK. I still got distracted intermittently but refocusing on my list of three tasks helped me. It's also really important to practise good self-care and ensure that you're getting enough sleep and proper nutrition.

Nothing good can come from giving in to moments of panic. Other than to understand that 'no action – is the best action' and to sit with the uncomfortable feeling until it passes. I have been triggered and I just have to keep telling myself, 'It's OK, just breathe'. I would think of something constructive to do in that time and accept that I shouldn't reach out to anyone for at least an hour and just do as much constructive stuff as possible.

Being self-aware is sometimes the hardest part of moving on but using that to be kind to yourself can be priceless.

Using my internal voice like a best friend again, I say things to myself like, *Something has really triggered you, hasn't it? You're panicking now. But it's all OK, nothing has changed, life hasn't changed. This new information or whatever the trigger was – was just that a trigger. Maybe you were comparing yourself, maybe you're feeling hurt. Just take it easy and be kind to yourself. This feeling will pass. You don't have to DO anything to let it pass. You don't have to make plans or contact anyone. Just recognize these rushing thoughts, observe them and let them pass with no action. Keep breathing. It will pass.*

Using your lists of priorities

Go back to previous chapters on lists that can help you keep focused. These items can't be solved immediately but can help ground your overwhelm and bring you back to the steps right in front of you. These lists will keep you productive, achieving, moving forward and feeling on top of the world and not under it. Before you know it, you will look at the clock, and find that the day has flown. You will be having a better day. Find a journal where you can write your lists and keep a highlighter pen at the ready. Then get stuck in.

You don't need to build Rome in a day. You just have to focus on your little bit for today. Work out what tasks need to be done right now, today and this week. What kind of things will you do for yourself, and what self-care tasks will you prioritize once this wobble is over? Using this simple practice, you won't lose a step in your strut to a better life.

These horrid feelings will stop over time. Getting on with things until that time has passed can only help you. Your life will get better from here.

Creating problems for yourself

I have learned to identify what my body is doing and stop my thoughts racing because sometimes, during moments of panic, I can do something that makes my life a million, no a gazillion times worse. Something would trigger me – and in response to the racing feeling that came from that, the adrenaline, the feeling of shock, I would seek out external comforters. That might be sending a panicky message to a friend or, worse, an angry message to The Ex, zoning out for an hour or eating an entire box of chocolates or doing other things not beneficial to me.

This is why calming and not panicking in the moment was so vital for me to learn, because once the overwhelm from the trigger has moved on, which can be as quick as a few minutes or even just an hour, the physical manifestation of that moment of overwhelm was more lasting and more damaging, as that moment had changed shape and was now out in the world. I couldn't just send another message that said, *'It's OK, just having a flap at the moment, please ignore.'* Once the actions of my panic were out there, there was no undoing it. I have made myself sick to undo the number of calories I had just consumed in a moment where I tried to use food to numb my mind. And messaging The Ex is never a good thing in any state. If I felt panicked before, waiting on a response or wondering whether they would even reply made me feel like I was sitting on needles. The feeling that I'd had when I sent the message had subsided, and the regret for my actions (caused by my feeling that I needed to do something at that moment) was so much worse.

When you feel that you're back at square one

One phrase that I have always heard from friends after a breakup, or I've said to myself when a relationship is ending or ended, is: 'I'm back at square one. All of this was for nothing. What a waste of my time.' There is this overwhelming feeling that you will have to go through this again. That all the past relationship battles and sacrifices were for nothing. You gave too much of yourself, your heart, time, headspace or money. The relationship was exhausting, and you don't want to ever go through that again.

What I have always told myself and others is to remember the fun and the good times when you first meet someone. such as:

- The first time you get that feeling that you like this person and then knowing they feel the same
- Being together and feeling that you have a connection.
- The excitement of planning things together

Are you actually back at square one? let's think about it. It is rare that the first partner that you meet and date is the person for you for the rest of your life. As a result you date and you get to learn skills around relationships but you breakup. Over time, you learn and grow as a person, the person you are with either grows with you or you grow away from each other. Dating new people brings a whole new dynamic and a raft of experiences that you may never have imagined. You have learned things about yourself in this relationship, you have learned and experienced new things because of this person in your life. You may crave familiarity after the breakup and want to go back to where you were, but now you get to experience so much more from life and better still a relationship that works for you and is a better fit for the person you are now.

Having a pity party

Sometimes when I have been derailed, I've treated myself to a pity party. By that, I mean spending however long I want to feel bad about whatever happened, but with a twist. I need to make it good fun for myself. I have used this to help snap friends out of their derailers too.

For example, I've had a bad day at work. I was late due to a collision or something that didn't go my way. I would say something like, 'Ugh, what a crap day, nothing is going right for me.'

Now, I could go full swing into giving up on having a good day, convincing my mind that all things are utterly awful, and this one event is the defining sign. But one way to snap yourself out of it is to have a jovial pity party.

For example, the statement 'nothing is going right for me'.

I might take a rational approach and say to myself, 'First of all, I disagree because actually, quite a lot was going right, it was just a bad couple of things happened, and I can't claim that as a result of a couple of bad things, everything is lost.'

But then I might decide to jovially agree with myself and validate how I felt but use a joking voice in my head.

Yes, you're right, nothing is going right for you, that one delay on the way to work and one meeting that didn't go well... well, that's ruined it all. Might as well leave town and join the circus now, not that they'd hire you. You aren't very good at your job, let alone the circus – you're not bendy, you can't catch, and you'd probably be eaten by a lion. Maybe you could sell candy floss. And don't forget you're single. You're a single circus reject...

What else is going wrong for you? Oh, that's right, you're a binge eating, single reject who should be shot into space as a replacement for chimps, but that's an insult to chimps. They've probably got their life together... Don't forget you've been ghosted on two dates. They didn't even need to meet you to realize that they didn't want to date you. They could sense it in the air.

I would make my statement in my head more and more insane, exaggerating why I had a good reason to cry or get sad. I always found that when I agreed with myself that I had a reason to be sad, it always snapped me right out of it. I didn't then carry on feeling bad for long. I had my little pity party to myself, had a laugh about it and moved on.

Sometimes a light-hearted pity party with yourself can be the best remedy for reminding you that things aren't as bad as they seem. So go ahead and laugh about it.

Dealing with shifting moods

My mood shifted day by day following the breakup with The Ex. It had been a few months, but my thoughts didn't seem to want to give it a rest. One day I was really high on life. I had woken up a totally different person and I could see the light at the end of the tunnel. But then the next day, I was down in the dumps again. I would send a search a probe into my brain to find thoughts or feelings left from the day before, maybe inspiration as to why that day had run so much better, but I was totally unable to recover my previous mood.

Whichever mood you're in, you feel that this is the mood that is forever present, and this is how it will always be from now on. If I was in a depressed mood, I would think, 'I have been depressed for months.' I would try to remind myself that I felt really good when I was out the day before and that this was temporary. But then my internal voice would say that I was, in fact, pretending and lying to myself on those days. I was depressed the day before; I just chose to pretend I wasn't.

When I was high on life, I could see that life was getting better and that I was indeed in a really good place. I could remember feeling low but felt in those moments that the dark cloud was now gone for good, and it would take something fairly catastrophic to bring me down. It was like Jekyll and Hyde with some normality in between.

What scale am I on emotionally at this minute?

The first step in controlling my breakup outcome was to recognize at any moment what level of emotion I was on. I noted that there were four in total. Each emotional level had different self-talk and actions to prevent me from derailing any hour, day or week. Following the breakup, I pinballed between any one of these emotions.

I labelled them:

1. Single buzz
2. The dumps
3. Zoned out
4. Normal me

Like Jekyll and Hyde, I found that my brain would not remember how to be sad when I was in the buzz phase. It felt as if I had recovered, that I could and would only ever see how great life would be. That I was attractive and desirable, and every moment felt precious, wonderful, fun. I would achieve the sweet spots having a BBQ in the park or staying out for the night with friends where we had the most wonderful fun times together.

When I was in 'the dumps', I believed that the single buzz person was made up in my mind, that I was only pretending and it was all fake. I could not believe that I could or would feel good without The Ex. I was boring, ugly and dull in all senses of the word. I had little to contribute to the world, and the world had little point.

In between, I would feel zoned out, where I didn't want to think or do anything, or I would feel like the normal me who wanted to keep doing things to keep myself on an even keel.

I wanted to document the different zones of emotion and the pros and cons of each.

1. Single buzz

Feelings: Exhilarated, amazing, euphoric, emotional high.

Statements I may think: I have one life I need to live. This person held me back. I'm free now. I'm unstoppable when I set my mind to it.

Actions I must not take in this emotion: Although this is one of the most motivating experiences and drivers for being single again, this can feel like a 'normal me' emotion but can sometimes create denial, leading me to do silly things. For example:

- Messaging The Ex to let him know how happy I am.
- Checking social media to prove I am happier than The Ex.

- Repeatedly posting on my own social media about how I'm over The Ex.
- Thanking all my friends who have been there for me in this difficult time.
- Hooking up with someone new and posting that to my social media.

Things to do: Enjoy it, use it and journal how you're feeling. You will need this for when you're in the dumps phase. Seeing information from yourself as to how good life is, is something you will need when you enter a depressed state.

2. The dumps

Feelings: Like my stomach had been torn out, hopeless, listless, fatigued, uninspired.

Statements I may think: Why bother, what's the point? It all goes wrong for me. how can I live without The Ex. All my relationships fail. I don't have anything going right for me. I am never going to meet anyone. I'm going to end up alone. I am not made for relationships.

Actions I must not take in this emotion: Believing that this is what I have always been feeling and what I will always feel. Texting The Ex, for example: 'Did you ever love me?' or 'Why are you doing this to me?' Looking at social media.

Things to do: Accept you're feeling low and sit in that feeling. It's OK to feel sad. If this feeling continues for a while, set a time to speak to a friend you can trust to listen and not just be there for the drama (do not have this conversation over text, they may be not paying attention), write to your best friend within and get the answer from them (see Chapter 3).

3. Zoned out

Feelings: Numb to the world and feeling nothing, no joy, no sadness. Purely existing. Groundhog Day.

Statements I may think: What was I working on? Where have I put my phone? Where did that time go? I have no motivation or focus. I don't even remember eating that. I'm so useless. What is the point?

Actions I must not take in this emotion: Remaining in it too long. Accepting it. Doing things that contribute to zoning out, such as buying ice cream/chocolate/alcohol, gambling, playing computer games, obsessing over social media, having one-night stand. Do not pick up a mobile phone to scroll to zone out.

Things to do: Create a list of actions to do each day. Start small. For example:

- Go for a walk. Look at the detail in the clouds, smell the air, listen to the sounds around you.
- Restrict screen time in exchange for something more physical and outward.
- Clean and tidy your home. Do nice jobs for yourself, which will benefit you when you come out of this phase and can help you get out of it.
- Plan activities with other people.

4. Normal me

Feelings: Feeling like I'm my normal/usual self, just getting on with things.

Statements I may think: I will meet someone right for me. I am doing well at work today. I am so glad I set out my clothes for myself. I look good today. I have been productive. A nice treat will be to watch a film with a nice meal.

Actions I must not take in this emotion: Doing things that can trigger you into another emotion. For example, you might think, 'I'm ok now, I think I can contact The Ex and be friends, I've moved on.' Checking The Ex's social media. Allowing in friends who like to talk about The Ex or give you emotional grenades. Dropping your guard by making small conversation and accidentally being sweeping statement bombed.

Things to do:

- Keep up the good habits by doing nice things for yourself, taking care of yourself, planning your outfits and maintaining good self-care practices such as exercising, eating well and feeling good physically.
- Keep a journal of how you feel to track the lows and highs, as well as when you just feel normal.
- Keep updating your goals and stick to achieving them. Again, having things to focus on keeps you moving forwards. Setting fun goals and not turning up for them will add to a low mood.

Menstrual cycle impact

A few days before my menstrual cycle, I am easier to be triggered than at other times. I have often been overtly offended by something or ferociously angry at things when I am within a few days of my cycle. This isn't giving any partner the permission to suggest that anytime I'm angry in this time frame, it is just my menstrual cycle. My anger is likely valid. However, I find sadness and anger more overwhelming. Also, when

I have been so low or embittered by things and then a few days later, my cycle comes, and I am less triggered. You may notice other patterns which trigger you.

Keep a journal

One of the main ways to keep sane after a breakup is to keep a diary or journal. This contains all of your daily ramblings, conversations with yourself and emotions. Journaling can become quite indulgent and self-pitying, so make sure it remains factual and focused. Try to write daily rather than just when you're in a low mood and want to talk with yourself. Otherwise, when you look through your journal, all you'll see is negativity.

Every day I recorded my true self because I wanted an accurate record of the fun I was having and how relaxed I felt. When the dumps hit me, I knew it was only a temporary emotion. Just keep the habit up. Keep going, and this will get easier.

Recording your good days as well as your bad days in your journal will help keep a more balanced view of how well you are doing when you look at your journal later.

In a nutshell

- Sometimes we get stuck in a negative frame of mind. We can choose how to interpret events around us. Look for the bright side and find humour in everyday life.
- Choose your mindset. Having a positive mindset can help you focus on the positives and draw more good stuff towards you.
- A negative mindset can distract you from seeing opportunities crossing your path.
- You may face a setback and feel like your mind is racing. In these moments, often the best action is no action. Breathe and remember: nothing needs to happen now, and this moment will pass.
- Acting out in a moment of unease can create more problems than it solves. Therefore not doing something to feel less out of control is the better course of action.
- Keep track of your moods and how they impact your willingness to take action or move on.

Get out your notebook

- Write down what you have done today as a comedy or a drama. Write down every detail for either type of your story.
- Now, look at the day you have had. Where could you have made it happier? Where could you have made it more joyful? If possible, keep this up for a few days and see if there is anything in your day that you can change your view on. Give an annoying event a comedy name.
- If you've had a bad day, have a pity party, including giving yourself some wonderful treats, like a movie you love, a drink you like or something else. Add on funny things to make the exercise fun – like a comedy straw in your drink.
- Write down happy goals each morning, where you can make a boring day more fun.
- Keep a journal of how you're feeling. Promise yourself that you're 100 per cent honest with yourself when you do this. You will journal on your good days as well as your bad to remember that you have many good and great days.

Sometimes you're ahead, sometimes you're behind, the race is long, and in the end, it's only with yourself.

—Baz Luhrmann

Chapter 9

The Bizarre Race to Move On

Sometimes the months following a breakup can feel like being in a bizarre race. A race to feel better, to not be left behind and to get over The Ex as soon as possible. It can feel like a race to meet someone new and move on before The Ex. It can also feel like a race against friends and acquaintances as if you have to try and catch up with what others have already achieved, or ensure you are not the last one off the shelf.

On reflection, it's daft to think that if you see your Ex with someone new in photos or hear from distant friends that they are dating again, that it automatically means they have moved on, and you're behind them. Relationships are complex. I thought I'd met "the one" with The Ex; after that crashed and burned who is to say his next partner would be any different. I had started to notice a few things, a few social truths that had not been apparent to me before. This race to move on is the effect of social competition and following by example. Let me explain with a story.

Like the story of *The Tortoise and the Hare*. You know the one, the hare and the tortoise are to have a race, the first one across the finish line wins.

The hare is smug in the idea that of course, a tortoise couldn't beat him, but then the hare decides to fall asleep, and when he wakes the tortoise has won the race.

In the same way, I knew I could spend the next five years looking like I was happy, settling down with the first good-enough guy that came along and taking a metaphorical nap. Changing my social media status to "in a relationship" and casting out photos of me and this person looking happy, pretend laughing for the photo. To The Ex (if they even wandered onto my social media, because of course all of these photos would be on public display) and the outside world, it would look like I had easily moved on.

The problem with settling down with someone who isn't a good match is that I would be less likely to meet his needs, or he mine. It would end because I didn't take the time to get to know him before I jumped in and decided we were in a relationship. I could lose years this way and not cross my finish line, which is meeting the guy I am meant to be with. Although I wanted to feel better from an outside perspective, showing others that I was happy by finding someone else really quickly, I knew playing this short game would lead me down a very unhappy path in the longer game.

When the whole point is to meet the 'one', it's a waste of time to start dating someone just because you don't want to be single.

I felt this massive pressure to meet someone. I had to keep reminding myself that I needed to wait for the right person, not the best right-now person. So from this perspective, I am like the tortoise. Whereas others are like the hare, they will get across the finish line, but there are quite a few diversions on the way they could have avoided. Although they think they have got across the finish line and will tell everyone so, only time will show you that they didn't. When their relationship ends and they are back in the race again.

Despite beating myself up for being single, I can speak from more experience now. At the time, I was shocked at how quickly people settled down. Now I can see that some of the relationships that looked perfect at the start, and made me envious, are the ones that failed down the road. They were, for the most part, the showiest of the relationships. Claims of marriage, lavish gifts and trips, engagements within months. As I've gotten older and more experienced, I wish I hadn't given myself such a hard time wondering why it never happened to me.

When I first met The Ex, his friend Ross had been with a girl called Jo for eight years. They had talked about getting married and having kids together. The only reason marriage and kids hadn't happened yet was that they were both saving and getting their careers in order first. Then Ross met a girl at work called Saroyan, who he just clicked with, he couldn't take his mind off her and couldn't wait until he had an opportunity to talk to her. He told me that she was stunning, the way she walked, dressed and talked. She had recently become single, so Ross talked to her and told her he liked her. She showed she was interested but said she would need a little time. Ross ended his relationship with Jo that evening.

It had taken Ross a month to get together with Saroyan. They would attend parties together, him saying he would marry her tomorrow if he could. She said how amazing fate was to bring them together. So loved up. However, my thoughts went to Jo, who must have been devastated. Eight years of relationship ended for her in one night. Jo took the breakup pretty hard, especially as she was fully aware Ross had started dating someone else so soon. She decided to not mix with Ross's friends even though she had made them a big part of her life for eight years.

Just after their first anniversary, Ross and Saroyan broke up. Saroyan ended it. She messaged me through social media about how vile Ross had been this whole time, that she wished she had never met him. A couple of years later Jo got married. Saroyan met another guy, and they also married a few years later and had two kids. Ross didn't marry. Several years later, he had a long-term girlfriend and a new baby. He was the last of the group to settle down.

My friend Mark experienced something similar when his three-year relationship ended. His Ex met someone else within six months, moved in with him, got engaged. He really struggled. He didn't date for the first year they were apart. He was quite broken after the breakup and even struggled to see himself with someone else after her. Sure enough, two years later, he moved to Australia, met someone and found happiness. His Ex broke up with the boy she moved in with, then spent the next few years going back to him until she made the break for good and took a few more years to meet someone new.

The path is unknown

In these situations, I'm not advocating for those who are single to be seen as failures and those in relationships to be seen as successes. Being in a relationship definitely does not mean that your life is fine and dandy and complete. Nor am I saying that those who make a lot of promises upfront are doomed to burn out, that whirlwind romances fail while those who wait are guaranteed a partner for life.

When I saw people settling down or being swept off their feet, I felt left behind. Their relationships seemed certain to last. Feeling unwanted,

I often asked myself, 'Why not me?' I spent so much time focusing on meeting someone and comparing myself to others unnecessarily. In the vast experience I have gained dating and being a single girl with a large bunch of female friends entering and exiting the single group, I found that many of the perfect and happy relationships I envied didn't last either. But we don't know where the path lies and where life will take us, that is the beauty and the pain of it. Many of these relationships still have a distance to travel – children, divorces and remarriages.

Do not compare yourself to others, you do not know what path their life – or yours – will take.

My single female friends and I have all gone through the period of frenzy of seeing The Ex posting a new relationship status or photo of a new girlfriend, captions with love hearts and people commenting things like "best couple ever!" As mentioned in Chapter 1, where we discussed how your brain likes to gather new information on The Ex to fill the void, and Chapter 5 where we cover making no contact with The Ex, by following The Ex on social media or by getting information via other means you are not helping yourself.

When I first split up from The Ex, I was keen to move on. But there was no rush. I would fall in love with the right person eventually. The Ex would also move on, and he would settle down himself eventually. I had many Exes, which this book is based on; each time I learned habits to move on and I got better at those habits. There is no competition 10 or 15 years down the road. This Ex will be a distant memory, like The Exes before them. You don't realize that at the start of the breakup, how unimportant this feeling will be many years down the line. The feeling that they are ahead and you are behind – none of this matters.

I doubt Jo thinks back to Ross or vice versa. I can only focus and could have only focused on my own path. The Ex was no longer part of my life, and as such, there was no tie to him. His happiness should not bring me sadness. His meeting someone made no difference to the timeline of when I would meet someone. I just had to take it in my own time.

Picking a better story

One of the main cues that upset me was the thought that I was a mess and The Ex wasn't. That the breakup had more of an impact on me than him. I convinced myself that I was the poor end of this breakup and that he was happier and better off without me. I would think about The Ex out with his mates, feeling good enough to meet a girl and being desirable enough to take her home. I would back up my assumptions by looking at his social media, seeing photos of him doing shots and talking to girls. It was obvious that he wasn't a mess like me. He, too, had lost weight but was looking pretty good. He had changed his look. I couldn't deny it. It looked good on him. I concluded – with this evidence to backed me up – he was doing better than me. He didn't miss me, and he is moving on.

But was he?

Do we ever take photos of ourselves questioning our life decisions and posting them on social media? Do we ever take photos of us missing someone, crying, annoyed or fed up?

Social media is simply content for cataloguing moments or check-ins you want to remember. On the whole, you wouldn't share moments you wouldn't want to remember. Maybe the extremes of something – 'look,

I got a flat tyre and had to walk home in the rain #badtimes,' but not, 'I opened a box of photos, and it reminded me of good times with The Ex, and now I'm crying, I ate a box of chocolates, which was good to zone out with, but now I feel even more miserable.' Nope. We wouldn't generally post stuff like that on social media.

I then looked at my social media. How did I look to the outside world? From an external viewpoint, I was looking good. I was out at club nights and had loads of friends making in-joke references on my feed. Photos showed me looking thin, tanned, involved, driven and even happy.

Then one day, I saw The Ex, and he looked awful. He didn't see me, he was just walking down the street, and I was driving past. He looked so wrapped up in his thoughts. A mirror image of how I would look at this present time. He looked really sad, it was a contrast to his clothes which were sharp and stylish, his hair was spiked and looking good, but he looked like a 10-year-old wearing his dad's clothing. It didn't match. He looked so sad. Now, of course, I don't know why he was looking so sad; he may have just got a speeding ticket in the post that day, or his gas bill was higher than expected. I had just a moment's glimpse of him.

I continued to drive down the street, ensuring I didn't crash into someone right in front of The Ex. I felt numb. I knew I would see The Ex at some point and thought whenever it would be, it might feel like a shock. I visualized him looking as if he was doing well when that happened. I didn't expect this. What was this feeling? I felt kind of good. Why? Some of it would be that I had now received information on the Ex. My brain was happy it had something to process – after periods without anything.

I didn't want him to be miserable. But it was good to think that his life wasn't perfect and wonderful. Now that was just a glimpse and what I took from that passing glimpse. He may have merely been thinking about something, and that was his resting face at that moment, like did I turn the oven off, where did I put that refund cheque. But I took it that his life was just like mine: having a good day in company with a mask for the outside, and hiding away sad days.

Importantly, my mood shifted. I felt like I was now off the hook to look happy 24/7. That it was OK to have an off day. I had chosen to run this script in my head that he was better off and happier, that this breakup didn't have an effect on him, when I had absolutely no evidence other than social media to back that up.

Seeing The Ex helped me realize that he may also be having off days. I'm not saying he was sad *because* of me, but it was a possibility that hadn't run through my mind. I was all supportive of the negative assumptions. Assumptions I had no proof were true, but I equally had no evidence suggesting he wasn't missing me terribly.

In the absence of knowledge, why not pick the more positive version of the events? Why go for the more negative one?

At that moment, I realized that nothing would change that we were over. Whatever happened in his day, month, and life was no longer my business. Whether his football team lost or he got a promotion shouldn't be a trigger for making my life better or worse. Equally, if he saw that I'd won the lottery and met someone new, that shouldn't impact him or his day either. We were no longer linked in life.

The bottom line is that it's not a competition with The Ex on who gets to be happy first. You can both be happy. *You'll get there,* I said to myself. *You'll get there.*

In a nutshell

- When you first split up, you may feel your Ex will move on before you, or you'll be behind others. In time you will know the bigger picture of how life goes for you and everyone around you. You're not behind or ahead. You're just living your life, and all will show itself in time.
- There is no rush to meet someone else. You will meet someone in your own time. It is better to be single looking for the right person than miss them because you were filling the gap with the wrong person.
- Often, we believe that others are so much stronger or doing so much better than us. We don't see their bad days. No one posts a day where they couldn't cope on social media.
- Don't tell yourself the Ex is doing better than you when you don't know; your Ex could be feeling awful. They would never tell you and you will never know their off days. Telling yourself this is just another way to make yourself feel bad.

Get out your notebook

- Make a list of the characteristics you define as successful. What characteristics do you define as happy and having it all?
- Now look at this list: how many of these things do you already have or do you already do, but you don't see yourself as successful? Which area of your life could you easily improve which would drastically change how you feel about yourself, what experiences could you also have? This might include unique nights out, taking a trip, experiencing a special meal or just your favourite pizza that you will enjoy unashamedly!
- There are things that you have that the people around you do not have. List all the great things you could share with others, great things you have going on in your life.
- If there are goals you class as successful that you want to achieve, write a list of objectives you could do this week, this month or this year which would make you feel more successful. It could be to complete a course, get more physically fit, run a 4k, make new friends, attend meet-up events or take pictures.
- Although social media does not reflect real life, posting things about your life showing the successful elements can make you feel more in control. Others may even look up to you the way you look up to others. This can be a great confidence boost. What can you post on social media to feel better about yourself? These photos can remind yourself that your life is just where it needs to be.
- Keep track of the great things you have done (and the things you're doing) in a journal or blog. Remind yourself of all the things that are going really well for you.

Advice: it's more fun to give than receive.

—Michael Forbes

Chapter 10

I'm Not Sick, I'm Single

Once you're single, you feel exposed when you share the information with others, as if the fact you're single must mean that you have personal problems or are a closet nutcase. People you meet in passing, extended family at gatherings or people you meet at work ask you whether you're in a relationship. If the answer is anything other than yes, you might notice this look creeps across their face. It's the intrigued look of them trying to work out what is broken about you. They say things like 'That's OK, you will meet someone,' or 'It's OK, you have time.'

One married colleague explained that there was no point going for a training course, as I wouldn't find men on it. I was shocked. I wanted to progress my career, not go on this course just to meet someone. The worst part is that you perpetuate this because when you're on the receiving end of "the look", you then feverishly try to explain why you're single as if you're late with homework: *I've been travelling, I work too many hours, I just don't have the time.* After which point, they leave you, and you find yourself slumped with a sigh.

I was even tempted to make up having a boyfriend. I thought it would just make my life easier. I'd name him Matt and imagine how great he would be and only bring him up when asked. That way, I'd always be seen as a professional woman, and no one could comment, privately or otherwise, on my private life. Thankfully this was just a passing thought.

It's not a level of success to be in a relationship

Not only that, but there are also women who treat their relationships like a degree certificate or a medal of honour. During the first few months after a breakup, it may feel like everyone in a relationship becomes an expert. They will explain the rules of how they made their relationship work, why they have managed to keep it together, and even what they feel you did wrong. This isn't generally meant to rub it in your face. It is more that they feel from their position as a person in a successful relationship that they are now fully qualified to advise those clearly devoid of the skill.

It is not a level of success to be in a relationship. These well-meaning people in relationships had not put in the work that I had put in. They had not earned it by being on hundreds of dates (like I had), they had been on a couple and as luck would have it, it just worked. I met guys who I grew incompatible with over time; sometimes it took weeks to months for us to realize it was going to work, sometimes it took months to years. Realizing that they did not want to spend the rest of their lives with me or I with them, should not be deemed as a failure on my part. But it seemed to be and it generally is seen as a failure.

I can't tell you the number of times women have told me stories of their partners as if they had trained them and become superior beings in their knowledge of people and relationships. They will describe why they got the ring the size of a golf ball, or how their partner gives them everything they need, as if I were missing a certain understanding of people and, more specifically, men. The reasons they told me included:

- You were too independent.
- You were too good at 'man' jobs, and they didn't feel needed.
- You've been spending too much time together.
- You moved in too soon.
- You didn't set enough boundaries.
- You had your guard up.
- You didn't plan enough trips together, or you had too many trips together.
- You let work come between you.
- You were too moody all the time (thanks, Mum).
- You were too tired all the time.
- I never liked them in the first place and never thought it would ever work. (Well, what can you say to that? Thanks, Dad!)

Some of these "reasons" were contributing factors. It's not like I lacked something, or I was a bad person, after all serial killers like Fred West, Ted Bundy and Gary Ridgeway were settled down and married. Being married or being in a relationship is not a sign that you're happy or successful, or that you have a special skill others do not possess.

I could change myself to perfectly fit into how someone wants me, or change how I live my life to stay with someone with different life ambitions or ideals, but let's face it, that wouldn't make me happy. Surely that's the biggest thing – are you both happy?

Relationships take work, but ultimately, you're either in it together, or you're not. The Ex and I were in the 'not' category. From time to time,

I thought maybe I was missing a trick because I was, in fact, single and appeared to have no immunity to that, but I just hadn't found the right person, that is all.

You know what your problem is/you know what you should do

My single life was a focal point of conversation when I met friends in relationships. Conversation would often move onto reflections of my strategy to secure a new partner and how this had to be improved, of course, with their expert knowledge. The advice I would get from friends ranged from where you can go to meet someone, to warnings that I was too keen or too 'hard to get', but the advice was usually along the following lines:

- You know what you should do, you should get out there and start dating.
- You know what you should do, you should take some time to yourself and get used to being on your own again, that way you can move on then meet someone.
- You know what you should do, you should have some time away, go travelling.
- You know what you should do, you should have a ton of flings and be selfish for a while,
- You know what you should do, you should focus on your career, forget the dating world for a while.
- You know what you should do, you should date online.

Once I had gotten through the list of 'should dos', then there were my problems:

- You know what your problem is, you're too independent, guys don't know what to do around you.
- You know what your problem is, you're too picky, if he's not perfect, you aren't interested.
- You know what your problem is, you haven't gotten over The Ex yet.
- You know what your problem is, you try too hard.
- You know what your problem is, you give the wrong guys a chance.
- You know what your problem is, you are too successful.
- You know what your problem is, you are too protective of yourself and keep your guard up.
- You know what your problem is, you are too open, you need to keep some of your life back and remain mysterious.

To be fair to my friends, they are all good people and love me. None of them wanted to see me unhappy. If I didn't deploy a subject change by using the three-line diversion (see Chapter 7), sometimes their advice and consoling were useful. I left, thanking them for listening to me and feeling a level of guilt that they must be bored of the topic by now. Other times things they said hit a nerve, sometimes because what they said was not helpful and was not thought through; these included comments like The Ex had moved on, that he had probably been cheating during our relationship or had been considering the breakup for a while. In the absence of any information to support this, I found this negativity difficult to stomach (covered in Chapter 7 and 8). Sometimes their advice was true and I found it hard to face the truth or they didn't realize that in my fragile state, comments that I could normally hear easily would cause me emotional pain. The most hurtful was their need to make me acknowledge that it didn't look like we were going to get back together.

Those giving advice could be getting it next

I didn't have a dating plan. I didn't have a plan on how I would have my happy ever after and meet someone. It's not like work, where you train, perform in your role and apply for the promotion. I could read every dating book in the land, but I couldn't predict when I would hit success and meet a match.

I would hunt for ideas and look at how others met their partners. If a friend said she met her new partner through speed dating, I would speed date. If I met some who focused on their hobbies, and then the right guy just landed in their lap, I would throw myself into my hobbies. I heard of someone that had three dates a week via different sources for six months, then met the guy. I decided I needed to increase my throughput of dates. A mate would never leave the house unless she was dressed impeccably and met someone in the pub. I started paying more attention to my clothes and wearing dresses out more often. I have to say that a nice fitting frock and heels really does improve your confidence. You are never caught out feeling like you look rough. But it was exhausting.

I was desperate for advice at this time, and by this, I mean gaining hope that others who had felt as hopeless as I did had gone on to meet the partner of their dreams. My one friend decided to focus on her career. She had decided to spend the next year getting to senior partner and being at the gym. This was all she focused on. She was in great shape, even with working 12-16–hour days. She met her match on a work night out. Now she's senior partner *and* with a lovely man. Take my advice, she said, just focus on yourself; that's the way to meet him.

Another friend took to dating like you would job hunting and dated methodically. She was on all the dating sites. She went to speed dating and salsa. She would push for nights out in busy social places like pitch and putt or golf. After eight months, she met the one. I don't think he fully appreciated how hard she looked for him. 'Take my advice,' she said, 'just be everywhere. Cast your net wide.'

Another friend met her happy-ever-after through a mutual friend at a house party. 'Take my advice,' she said, 'accept any house party invites. You can get to know your friends better. Don't go to nightclubs, as the partner you'll want to meet will likely be like your friends.'

Others advised me to take a break from dating and 'just be'. This sounds great, but deep down, I'd be using my 'just being' as another way to meet someone, remembering the line, 'You'll find him where you least expect it.' But this theory didn't hold water. I was least expecting it every day. Some days I went out 'least expecting it' with a full face of makeup even though I was just going to the shops or going furniture shopping with my mum.

I was told to 'Always be ready as you never know when you'll meet him,' but technically, does that mean I am no longer 'least expecting it'? Hence wearing makeup created bad luck because now I was expecting it. Then that creates problems because if I didn't wear makeup and met the one whilst 'least expecting it', I might lack the confidence of feeling like I was ready. Either way, the rules to meet a man changed every time I spoke to someone new.

Engaging in the rules

I felt like all I ever seemed to do was listen to other people's success stories on meeting their life partners. Every time I tried these so-called tactics myself, I didn't meet anyone. However, suddenly, these were the ways to 'meet someone' by someone else's standards.

I met quite a lot of people all the time. There appear to be two types of people you hang out with when you are single. The first group is made up of fellow single people who you go clubbing and drinking with, and join for any random activity from new sports (in my case golf) to a local mindfulness and yoga class.

The other people I would hang out with were reformed single friends in newly formed relationships of around a year. These women still wanted to go out and have some independence from their partners. Meeting up with the new boyfriend was still pretty much dates and making plans, as opposed to those in longer-term relationships, who from my experience truly understood that Fridays are for takeaways, wine and PJs – not for hitting the town with your girlfriends.

However, in the society of women, these ladies with the new boyfriends, who were saying *I love you* for the first time, having the most amazing romantic dates and regularly receiving flowers, became the group leaders on how to get a boyfriend and keep one. I constantly heard various areas of theory and myth. I will run through the main ones unpick them below.

- Treat them mean, keep them keen.
    - I do not advocate for being mean to anyone. This one I have never understood. A date is never going to understand why you are being mean and want to be with a mean person in the longer term. If they do, then they are setting themselves for a drastically unhappy relationship.
- Always be looking your best, check your make-up in the mornings, look drop-dead gorgeous on dates.

  - I believe you can only be you on a date. If what you wear makes you feel uncomfortable than that will show and reduce your confidence. You need to be the most confident you, that you can be. I always went on dates feeling my best, whether on that day it was in jeans or a dress. If I felt I wanted extra makeup and more hair styling time, that is what I did. It's about presenting the best version of you, not presenting something you are not.

- Don't fit them into your diary when they ask. Make them wait.
  - I have noticed we are more and more in a disposable culture. If you put others first, you will teach them that you come second. If you make yourself available to dates (and friends for that matter) they get used to you being readily available. If later down the road you want to work things around time frames that better suit you, dates or friends wonder what has changed and why. This is a boundary I have learned to use. It's not about pushing them away, putting them off or being difficult. If I was free and it was convenient I would meet up. I was so keen to see some dates that I would literally try to fit them in when it was an inconvenience to me and difficult for me to fit in. This then became a normal situation for them, that I would fit to their schedule.

- Don't respond to their messages for a day or two.
  - I am a believer that "I cannot miss you, if you do not go away". Similar to what I discussed above around my availability for dates, I didn't want to be readily available by text or Whatsapp but would text when I was free. Sometimes I struggled with this more than my date! I had often pulled

over on the roadside when I was driving so that I could reply to a text message. This happened over 5 times on one journey. The date could have waited until I got home, but I was too keen to message back. Waiting that small amount of time would have allowed for a better conversation and maybe heightened his anticipation of hearing from me.

- Don't text again if they haven't replied. (This is good advice.)
    - If someone hasn't replied to your first message they are unlikely to reply to your second message.
- Don't let him stay over.
    - This is personal preference. Again, I think it's good to miss someone and have that distance and anticipation. I like to get to know someone. Also, I am safety conscious about having strange people in my home alone and going to their home alone.
- Don't appear to overly like them. Keep them guessing.
    - I had a date who couldn't tell if I liked him, I had a date who said I seemed over keen. I have had friends say they had a date who made them feel really confident and it settled them into the date. Others have said excessive compliments put them off. I think it's OK to show you like someone, but be measured. There is a group of guys guided by toxic masculinity who have openly written in books to make passive negative comments to a girl to make her feel bad, that way you have a better chance of bedding her. This line of thinking disgusts me. I did meet a guy in a bar who tried this tactic on me. Everything he said was a thinly veiled slight. I would rather have someone just happy to be in my company.

- Set the rules from date one. You don't want to be walked over.
    - As mentioned above, I have learned over time that whatever I do at the start, people expect from that day forward. I became more realistic on my time to save more for me and what I needed to do.

I liked to be me on dates. If a date texted, I would text back as soon as I was able. If they asked when I was available, I would tell them the next slot in my schedule. On some dates, I'd get dressed up, while others would be more casual. If they wanted a no effort date at the pub, cafe or eventually at one of our homes once I had gotten to know them, that was OK. This was not the right way of doing it, according to my friends with new boyfriends.

As these friends had successfully found a mate, but not just that, mates who seemed to worship them, I felt obliged to listen to them. As I am single I obviously know nothing about dating, how to hold down a relationship or how to make someone happy. I even compared notes with other single girls. I'd state, 'Well, Joanne did this, she's been with Tom for eight months now, and he's bought her flowers and taken her on surprise dates, she obviously knows what she's doing. I need to be more like Joanne.' The following month it would be Sarah's advice. 'Well, Sarah did this. She's been with Dave for a year now. He took her to Venice for their first anniversary. I need to be more like Sarah.'

Each time I went out or messaged someone via one of the various dating websites (which means loads of them, even the little obscure dating sites), I would run through these rules in my head. This is what I need to follow to jump ship from this single lifeboat to the big ship of relationship.

It seemed that if I didn't find a man, surely this would be because of how I was playing the game. I decided if I'm good fun and present myself in an unattainable and mysterious yet attractive way, surely that is the solution to my relationship issues. For a month, I went on this way, and I became someone I am not: not replying to guys I liked, making it difficult to set a date, being off and bossy.

I would meet up with Joanne and Sarah, amazed at how they continued to have romantic dinners with their boyfriends, swishing off on a romantic break away. Until one day, one or both of them broke up.

When this type of breakup comes, it's always totally out of the blue to me. However, Joanne and Sarah will tell you it's been coming for a while. They weren't actually truly happy. They were lying to themselves, becoming frustrated with the boyfriend. He wasn't that great after all, and the romantic dates were mostly planned by them or hinted at. He didn't want to put the effort in. They are relieved to be single and be able to find themselves again because he took up too much of their time. They wish they hadn't bothered with him in the first place, it was clear from the start it wasn't going anywhere.

At this point, Vicky or Claire pipe up that Joanne and Sarah should take their advice as they are in a happy 13-month relationship with their partner, and they were more relaxed about it. They were, in fact, single for a long time before they met these guys, and they believe that did them a world of good and will lead to meeting a better match and not wasting your time. Also, all these rules made it difficult for the guys. Vicky and Claire didn't follow the rules of playing hard to get. We decide we need to be more like Vicky and Claire and stay single for a while. I need to be more chilled with these guys and less high maintenance. I've been doing it all wrong. If I'm more chilled, *then* I will be saved from my lifeboat of single! Until Claire and Vicky split from their partners, then it was onto the next guru.

You need to meet a perfect match who work well together with you. Do not change to be what you think they want.

In following all this advice, I wasn't paying attention to the long-term. By that, I mean all these people had experienced success, and I tried to copy what they did, but then what they did would fail at some point or (like me) they would have a conflict of confidence about things and whether this was working for them after all. Ultimately, the aim is just to meet someone and for them to like me for me. Not because I didn't reply to messages or was bossy.

There was no real strategy in the end, just finding ways to meet people, doing things that I liked to do, or living my everyday life. The more you are out there to meet people the higher the likelihood of coming across someone you are compatible with. It's that simple. Sometimes you may feel like you're losing the race, sometimes you're winning. In reality... who cares? What matters is, are you happy? Part of being happy is ignoring what you think being single means and starting to enjoy what a single life brings.

Pretending to be someone else when dating means they may not meet the real you.

Thinking about what others think

When you're in a relationship, you're immune to many people making mean comments. For example, I have friends who referred to someone they didn't like and said, 'Yeah, well, she's single. That's because no one likes her.' The single friends would be massively embittered if the girl they didn't like was in a stable, loving relationship, and they would be overjoyed when it all came crashing down. The number of times that girls have said to me something like, 'Gosh, *[insert name of the person they didn't like]* is single, even he couldn't put up with her. Her boyfriend finally saw her true colours.'

I didn't believe for one second that I was immune. Although I believe I am a good person, I Imagined a few people I have crossed paths with over the years, having a field day learning that I had split up and was now single again. When The Ex and I were having conversations about working on the relationship as we recognized we were drifting apart, I worried about all the people who would be chuffed to bits to know that no one loved me if our relationship failed. Some of the people that popped into my head I hadn't seen in over a decade. I doubt any conversation about the fact that I was single would have lasted more than a minute and a half or that the news would ever even get to them. Yet, it was weirdly the thought that bothered me.

With hindsight, I can see how silly it is that I stayed in a relationship longer than I should just to prove something to the outside world. That I fought to stay with the wrong person due to the shame of my relationship failing. The only thing I proved was that I could delay myself from happiness due to the unknown view of people who didn't exist in my life. How pathetic was that? I also considered other things I have held back on because of disapproving comments or snarls of disdain from my haters. How sad that I let these thoughts ever hold me back.

I'm not going to pretend that I haven't been semi pleased when a girl who has purposefully tried to hurt me has received her end of karma. The very fact that she is single confirms to you that she must be a horrid person after all and that even her boyfriend, fiancé or husband cannot bear her. But I am also a mix of jealousy and admiration when her life rockets. I saw one girl I lost touch with launch her own health, fitness and nutrition business. She was single now with two small kids. I bet that it was hard pushing through her self-doubt to become such a success. I was so happy for her but it was tinged with jealousy rather than hatred. She met someone a few years later, and everyone was so amazingly happy for her when she got engaged. Yet when she had launched her new business website the year before, things were quieter on her social media. There were quite a few congratulations, but people were more reserved around her business than her engagement. It frustrated me that her success was seen in having the business and the man, or just the man. Being successful and single isn't always seen by others as a complete picture, rarely is the single woman with the great business seen as a success.

Being set up

Some people really cannot stand to see you single. My mother was one of them. I was invited to a family friend's wedding only to find that my mother had already had a conversation with her friend scoping which prospective single men would be attending. It was so embarrassing. It didn't matter how hard I tried to establish a boundary about being set up. It would always happen. Once it was just a man going about his day selling double glazing who happened to knock on the door. She showed him my university photo on the wall and took his business card.

I had friends who meant well too. They set me up with a guy who was really not my type. But I gave them credit that he was at least a nice guy. The kind of guy I wished I would like, I bet he would treat his girlfriend so well, but I didn't feel a spark. However, it wasn't always understandable. Sometimes I felt as though I was being sent off onto the single table and that couples didn't want to hang out with the single girl for too long.

What I hated was that, to some degree, they were right. I went to most events hoping to find a potential partner there. I did that with pretty much every night out or event. At the end of the day, you have to meet people to meet someone. So these were key events to do just that. But I didn't want other people to think that as well. I wanted to attend and check out the attendees myself for potential boyfriends rather than someone having that agenda for me.

Thankfully, friends didn't do it too often, and I had to accept that my mum would do it whether I liked it or not. I just made a point to leave early – once I checked for myself that there weren't any single guys who were my type there, obviously.

Feeling like so much time has been lost

If I spent every night for the next year working on my career, taking courses trying to advance myself and taking on more responsibilities, there is a good chance that I may start getting recognition. I have worked towards qualifications needed by my employer, and I will likely receive a promotion. It's not guaranteed, but with the right work in the right place, I can make a difference in my outcome. If I put all my heart and soul into my relationship with someone, giving them the majority of my evenings and weekends, being kind and thoughtful, going out of my way to think of events we can attend together, sharing my heart with them and listening to their needs, the relationship may still fail. I can try to put the right work in the right place, but there is no guarantee that others will do the same. I may meet all their needs working on the relationship, but they may not meet any of mine.

I have had relationships where I've played hard to get, and the guy chased me, and ones where I appear to be doing most of the work. Both times the relationship has ended. I was, however, most gutted at the relationships where I felt I had really put in a lot of effort to keep the relationship good. Not so gutted about the ones I felt casual towards, even though those lasted a good amount of time. I sometimes convinced myself that the best way to keep a relationship was to care as little as possible and be as casual as possible. In time I realized how ridiculous that was. I was losing little heart but a lot of time on people who wouldn't hurt me but were never going to be long-term prospects.

As a woman, I felt that once I was over 30, there was biological pressure to meet someone and settle down. The fairy-tale futures I had designed in my head since a child, likely put there by Ken and Barbie and numerous animated films, suggesting that all princesses needed was a prince, all pointed to being married by 30. So I wondered how I had passed this number and was not living happily ever after yet! Working harder wasn't the answer but finding someone who wanted to work with me in the longer term was. Casual relationships were not the answer.

Wanting to know what the future had in store

At different points after the breakup, I sought advice from any possible source on what the future held for me. I wanted to see a medium to give me an idea of what was coming next. I would ask a question out loud, saying, "the next song will give me an answer to what I need to do to meet someone new this year," then intensely listen to song lyrics trying to decipher my answer from the universe. It would be some song telling me to put my hands in the air or some other unrelated topic.

I read my horoscope, I attended church wondering if the sermon would be aimed at me (even though I am not Christian and do not attend church normally). I have bought decks of cards from Angel to Tarot, asked the deck a question, picked a card then tried to interpret an answer. Maybe I should flick this book to a random page, and it will land on the answer. Finally, where is that magic 8 ball I had as a novelty gift a few years back?!

If someone had told me at this point a mystic muffin would give me the answer to my questions if I took a bite and spread the crumbs, I would have visited every bakery in town to find it. I struggled with whether my actions whilst with The Ex were right and all my actions since we split up were right:

- Was I doing all the right things trying to meet someone new?
- Were The Ex and I meant to be?
- Should I be fighting for him?
- Should I be letting him come back to me when he is ready?
- Should I be calling him or leaving him alone to miss me?

It seemed no matter how much I thought what I was doing was right, at the same time, it also all felt very wrong. I can't say that any of my actions or feelings felt natural. My mind was bouncing all over the place. Some days I'd feel that I was pretty much in control, that it was all OK. Another day I would feel as if my life had been derailed, and this wasn't 'supposed to happen'. Only time would tell. In a few years from now, I would know the answer, and that would be that.

I decided to write out my own horoscope as a bit of a joke at first, but then I really got into it. If I could create any future for myself, what would it look like? I wrote that I focused on my career and had an active social life. That I would come into my own that year and flourish. That I would get an amazing apartment of my own and live a life I had previously dreamed about. That life could be easy if I let it be. That I would learn skills that would help me stop being the source of my own emotional pain. I didn't know where some of these ideas were coming from, but it felt lovely to read at times that I felt lost.

A friend gave me some really great advice. She said, 'Whether you're with him or not, time will decide. You'll either find your way back to each other – or you won't. It's not fate. If you can work it out as a couple to stay together, you will. If you can't, then you won't. The next guy you fall in love with won't be down to fate. It is just by chance you met a person, and that person was compatible with what you want. You work together. It will last if you continue to do that and fail if you don't.'

When you learn to swim, to prevent drowning, one of the best manoeuvres you can do is to breathe deep, lie back and just float on the water's surface. You aren't flailing around or exerting any energy. You just lie back, keep breathing, and in time, help will come. I think this is a great metaphor for life and difficult times. Just keep breathing and keep floating. In time, this will pass.

What I decided was, in life, I can be anything I want to be. There was no point wondering if I would meet someone. I knew deep down it would all be ok, I just needed to focus on what I wanted from life (covered in chapter 2) and let the rest sort itself out.

The trick is to follow the river course of life and not worry too much. You can only be who you are at the moment, do your best and hope for the best. The rest will work out, but it's not in your power.

In a nutshell

- Many people might be giving you advice, but remember, it isn't a level of success to be in a relationship. You don't achieve relationship status following training. It's just that some people have met someone they can work with, and you're still looking for yours.
- You may try everything people suggest to meet someone and still not meet your next partner in these places. Although it's always good to increase opportunities to meet people, don't put too much pressure on yourself.
- Advice can be useful, but you have to be yourself. You can't pretend to be someone else or act like someone you're not.
- Although you may feel uncomfortable being single, remember that having the freedom to meet the right person is better than being in the wrong relationship.
- Know that, in time, things will work themselves out.

Get out your notebook

- Write down an action list of all the places you can meet people who may have similar interests to you, e.g. book club, variety of sports clubs, single person adventure holiday, speed dating, online websites, online events. Then get out there and join those groups.
- Write down your own horoscope. Predict the great things that are going to happen for you within the year. You can add this to the tasks in Chapter 2.
- Put positive or powerful statements on pieces of paper, then fold them up and put them in a jar or box. When you feel low, pick one out as a statement which is attuned to what you need to hear at that time.

Friends are people you meet on the journey. Some only for a stop or two, some get off and rejoin, the very precious last the whole ride. But each is valuable as they were all part of the journey.

Chapter 11

Friendships and Singledom

So I was out dating again. I was going on date after date. I'd have that one date in a pile of rubbish ones, where I thought, wow, that's a nice guy. We would have a second date and a third date. Things would be going well. It would be no promise of long-term, but it was nice. It had potential. I had hope again, hope that I would have a relationship and things would and could work. When you start to move from just dating to that pre-boyfriend/girlfriend state you have to deal with a lot of single girl politics. Which I can never get my head to understand, but it's worth knowing about. I find single women have the most bizarre lists of rules and they will get angry if you break any of them.

I will say in advance of all of this, that it's not worth letting your friends upset you or let it impact you, you just have to accept what happens with a pinch of salt and a deep breath, and try to ignore it.

Handling Jealousy

Now, during my time when I was single, I'd say there are three types of single women:

1. Those who can be genuinely happy for you that you're dating someone new.
2. Those who are kind of happy for you but have that jealous feeling that they wanted it to be them.
3. Those who treat the fact that you have a new boyfriend like you have stolen away from their opportunity to meet someone. As if the fact that someone who was once single has taken their ticket in the line to meet someone.

Well, hand on heart, I'd say I'm somewhere between one and two, when a friend found a new guy in my single days. I was genuinely happy, especially when the guy was really good for them and supportive. There was also a part of me that ached a little because I wanted it too.

Then there are the times when friends pick up on something you say about your new date that *they* don't like. They may say something such as "Ew, I couldn't date someone with that hair", "Ew, not a body builder, who wants someone who is in the gym all day", " I couldn't date someone that works long hours like that, workaholic or what". I really hated this because it made me feel that they were insulting the guy I really liked. Also, it made me question (only for a moment) whether I was all hopeful about a guy who was not good for me, or would let me down somehow. As if my friends could see something I was blinkered to.

I realised the friends saying such things were only doing so because they were jealous of what I was developing with this guy and they had to find a reason why it wasn't a good prospect in order to stop their feelings of jealousy.

One time, it happened for one of my long-term single friends in our group of single friends. I was overjoyed for Emma. The new guy was really a top-notch bloke, made an effort for her, funny, thoughtful, good worth ethic and good looking. The kind of guy a single girl assumes is a mirage in the desert. My friend, gentle, sweet, thoughtful, petite, blonde and beautiful, was getting to a serious point and was happy. She brought him to our friend's birthday to meet us. We had a lovely meal with Emma and Nick. He ended up being the only guy at the table, but he shared stories, laughed with us, bought the birthday girl a drink and, all in all, was a lovely addition to the group.

I'm sad to say that the birthday girl, Alexis, was well into the third category of single women, who took it as a personal insult that Emma was with someone. That night, all I heard from Alexis was how Emma only brought Nick along to rub it in her face. Rub it in all our faces that she had met this guy and we hadn't, that Emma just wanted to flaunt it and should have known this would ruin her birthday. In fact, they fell out for a while after. Emma and Nick split up several months later because that's how it goes sometimes, and suddenly Alexis and Emma could be good friends again. I don't think that Alexis is a bad person. She couldn't stand that Emma had met someone and she hadn't yet. Once Emma was single again, she was no longer competing for happiness. Which was daft, really, as now she was single again, technically they were looking in the same pool of guys for boyfriends. Alexis didn't get that. Yes, Nick was a good guy. However, he wasn't someone she wanted to date. So where was the competition? She would never admit it, but it was jealousy. When the shoe was on the other foot, Alexis met a new guy while we were all still single. Alexis didn't come to the meal and spent the night with her new boyfriend. This is also acceptable, but I'd prefer the more, the merrier, rather than cancelling.

In fact, when I looked around my best friends who have husbands and babies – everything I wanted for myself – I didn't fancy their blokes either. My friends being in relationships wasn't stealing men from my pool of potential mates. They made the water clearer, so there was no competition. I acknowledged they hadn't taken anything away from me. They hadn't taken a guy who would complete my life, so why feel jealous or bitter. I wanted what they had but not in the way they had it. They were not my competition. In the same way, I can attend weddings, and apart from dealing with the 'being single is a disease' issue, I can still be happy for my best friends who have found love.

When I met someone, I felt this weird vibe from some of my friends. As soon as you meet someone and start to want to spend time with someone, some friends can be quite off with you. They can give you a hard time, stating that "you have ditched them for the guy", "only using them to meet someone", or even "it's ok for you, you've met someone". I was still seeing my friends but not as frequently as I would before, but I was splitting my free time. It can be quite hypocritical as the same people will also wish to cancel plans when they are dating. I never minded a friend taking time away from the group when she met someone. Just accept that your friend group may get tetchy, you do not have to give in to their pushiness. I was deleted as a friend once for saying I couldn't make a night out, that is how petty it got for me personally. I tried my hardest to take it as a compliment that they liked my company when we were out.

The ones that like to save face

I am a very honest person. If I have been rejected by a guy, I share the details of what happened with my friends. I thought that was what other people did. I thought we were all vulnerable with each other. It just seemed that I had more negative stories. I thought it was me. My friends seem to only talk about complimentary emails from guys.

My friend Siobhan had just come out of a relationship with her fiancé of two years. He begged her to go back, but she wasn't having any of it. She had met someone else since the breakup and told me that she had said to her Ex how much better off she was now. She told me the only way to get The Ex to come begging back was to not feed his ego. She said, 'Tell him what a waste of space he is and how he's short and balding. He'll get off his high horse after that and realize he's losing a good thing. That's how you do it. You put them down and put yourself on a pedestal. You are the best they will ever have. Then they have to come back to you because they will think they can get no one else. Then don't text them; they will text you.'

I don't have it in me to list someone's bad points. I assume that if someone doesn't want to date me, then telling them how ugly they are will not make them want to be around me. But this worked for her. I questioned whether I was a pushover and not putting myself on a pedestal enough; these men should worship me – perhaps that was why I was single

A few months later, I bumped into Siobhan's ex-fiancé. He was a friendly guy. He looked uncomfortable when he saw me but made an effort to say hello. I said I was sorry that he and Siobhan ended and asked him how he was doing. He said he found it hard, as she was always texting him, begging him to come back and asking if she dumped her current boyfriend whether he would take her back and marry her. She had lied. She had sent the odd nasty text, but a couple of days later, she apparently would always call saying she was sorry. He said she really knocked his self-confidence, and he couldn't be with someone who wanted to dominate and drag him down.

That's the thing about advice. You have to take it in, think about it, but most importantly, see if it actually applies to you; one rule doesn't fit all. I had to be myself. Something I have come to learn is that there is no expert at being you in a relationship.

Cut yourself and your friends some slack with how you act and what you say, accept people for their frame of mind at this point of life and just enjoy their company.

We need friends at every stage of life

I met quite a large number of single girls when I became single. We went out frequently, trying the new bars and great clubs. We even went on a couple of girlie weekends and holidays. When we were in that phase, it was so much fun. It was a good way to keep busy, have company and get ourselves out and about in the hope of meeting someone. At the time, I thought this time was mostly about making friendships.

Those left on the journey can get bitter at those leaving. Some leave and then rejoin later. As for me, I believed the more, the merrier. Others in our group didn't want people rejoining a ship they'd deserted to investigate greener pastures.

However, as only a small number have remained in touch with those who were in the group, I know that the group had a limited purpose. We kept each other company on the journey.

I observed the group's self-esteem go up and down, as well as the interactions and dynamics of this group of women. These women went from relationship to relationship throughout our friendship. All eventually settled down into long-term relationships, some with marriages, some with babies, some with both. I believe friendships form when people come together with a common purpose or function; ours was to not be stuck at home alone and we served that purpose for each other. I don't believe that these women are the same people I met back then. I think they wanted to meet someone and the group helped keep them motivated and positive amid the difficulties of dating.

I think I spent a good amount of time stressing over my friendships and the fallouts. We were all challenged by our self-esteem, questioning our route in life, and wondering what was in store. I should have just accepted the fall outs as par for the course.

Being single and finding out who you are as an adult is a life stage, so forgive the bickering, petty fights and fallouts that happen among your single friendship groups.

I realized that I had to accept that each stage of life had its people. During school, I had peers, a small number of whom I am friends with 30 years later. Then came colleague friends, apprenticeship or first job friends. Then next job friends and hobby friends; partner's friends and family; and if you have kids their friends' parents and their hobby friends' parents. Along the way, we have a fair number of friends and acquaintances, some of whom will stay the course of your life.

For some reason, single friends tend to be more possessive than friends you meet at other stages of life. I've often heard things like 'as soon as she meets a guy, she's gone' or 'she's only messaging because they broke up.' The fact is that was true at times for all of us. Some are just more subtle about it than others. Other friends are a total liability and will ditch you on a night out or make plans but always cancel shortly before, not giving you any way to make new plans and recover your evening. Those people are different. If you're left in the middle of a club on your own and worried about getting home, or they never come out and always cancel, it's probably not a good idea to rely on them. These are not friends. You are not a neatly packaged single use 'friend' sachet for them to use when they need someone.

I had one friend who, a year into her relationship, informed me that she had moved on from our friendship now that she had settled down and so would not be coming out with us anymore, opting for her boyfriend's friend group. I understood that she wasn't going to be coming clubbing with us any day soon, but to have been moved on from felt a little brutal. At the two-year mark, that relationship broke down, and she wanted to have friends around her. Many didn't want to be there for her. I understand that we have different priorities from time to time and cannot be the same people. If I were going for a promotion at work, I wouldn't want to spend Saturday and Sunday in the pub only to rock up to work on a Monday morning, exhausted from my social life. I might cool it down a bit and even work at weekends. As a friend, I wouldn't expect people to call me out on that. In the same vein, I wouldn't inform my friends that I'm only hanging out with work friends. Life is a cycle; you meet people, you lose touch, and then you're inseparable, and then you don't see each other for a while. We don't need to define people or define stages of our lives. When I have kids, I may not see my female friends so much anymore, but it doesn't mean that the one time I'm able to have a child-free night, I drop everything and party with my best friends. The ones who know my old story, my current story and are desperate to hear the next story will know that we'll find time for each other. People are not clothing or single-use plastics.

So, for the most part, I learned to accept people for where they were. If they were good fun and I could get out and have a good time, I didn't worry if they didn't have long-term ideas about our friendship. I didn't over-invest in them, and I didn't expect them to over-invest in me. I enjoyed the company when I had it, and I'm still best friends with many of them 15 years down the line.

Avoid believing that friendships with other singles are created in the fire as if we are a tribe of women that put the men aside for each other. It's just not the case, and we have to accept that. Sometimes you will keep that friendship, and sometimes you won't. There is no way of knowing which people will stick with you for the long-term.

In a nutshell

- When you're single and have a close-knit friend group, its dynamics may be up and down. You may all be having different issues around self-esteem.
- Some friends may focus attention on the group, wanting to be the first to meet someone or have the best relationship. Accept that that is what they need to do.
- Some friends will see the group less when they meet a new love interest. Accept they're happy in a new relationship. They can do their thing, you can do yours; if it all works out, you'll be there on their wedding day or child's first birthday. They don't need to give you all their free time to be friends.
- Some people have little thought for you. These people who will leave you on a night out may cancel too many times. Some people are unsafe. These are not friends.

Get out your notebook

- Write down something you would like to do next weekend, next month or next year (this may be from previous chapters).
- Now write next to it the friends: 1) who are up for it with you; 2) who would encourage you to do it; 3) who would dismiss it or make you question your choice; and 4) who would probably not respond to the message.
- Now write down a list of friends who would 1) be happy if you met someone, 2) be happy but weird and 3) start to become frustrated quickly that you are not available for meet-ups.
- Now looking at the two lists, there will be friends who would support you with a new partner but are not likely to join your plans, and there are friends who would join you on great adventure plans but be jealous and difficult when you meet someone. Both sets of friends are there for you but in different ways.

You don't need every date to fall in love with you. You just need the right one.

Chapter 12

Dating

I had to be honest with myself when an attractive guy at work sent my brain into a chemical tizzy. I could call it fancying, a crush, an infatuation and just lust. He was in a group photo with me and others. Gosh, I couldn't count the number of times I looked at the photo. I'd just look at it and have these butterflies because I really liked him. Short bursts of eye contact with him would send my brain into overload, wondering what it meant and whether he thought the same way. When he opted to be on my team, I wondered if it was because of me.

I have had some crushes reciprocated and some that clearly weren't. When I have gotten together with a crush, the feeling has been amazing and tortured. My brain was doused in good feeling when I was with them and missing it when I wasn't. I wanted to be with them all the time as a result. I was getting to know them, and sometimes, I would find something that I really didn't like about them. Where their values and mine didn't meet, the good chemical feeling would stop flowing. Also, there have been times when the good feeling had clearly stopped on their side. They had switched off because something was incompatible in an area intrinsic to their being, and once that has been switched off, it's pretty impossible to switch back on again.

Should you let that stop you from enjoying the feeling? No! it may not be reciprocated, but you don't have to put a dampener on the lovely exciting feelings. I have had crushes on guys that I knew I could never date for whatever reason, such as they were too young for me, or they wished to live in a different country and I didn't at that time, or they clearly didn't fancy me. I still enjoyed being in their company. Enjoy the good vibes and feelings. Don't take everything to heart.

Digital dating

For me, online dating and speed dating is one way to numb the overwhelming feeling of being helplessly single. You have to fill your mind with something, whether it be a passion for your job, your kids, your hobby or your partner. In the absence of that person, in the absence of being loved by someone, I needed something to focus on and some way to feel like I was moving forward. So before long, I found myself on various dating websites and speed dating so often that the sheer number of male faces I viewed monthly must have been in the hundreds.

Between my friends and I, there are three schools of thought for single people:

1. Those who feel they need to work on themselves and be single for a while before they can date.
2. Those who are very selective on who they date and only date a limited number of people.
3. Those who date a range of guys – it's a numbers game, after all.

The fact is you only need to meet one. Not eight, not 1000 but that one. Some people can meet that one at school, others wait most of their adult lives. I had been through tons of dates online and hadn't met anyone, meanwhile one of my best mates dated one guy, one! He was her absolute match on every level. By that 'one,' I am not saying that each person has one person they can ever be compatible with. But when you meet someone who connects with you and meets your needs, you stop looking. There could be many 'ones' out there. You just have to meet the one you feel for, and who feels the same for you.

You might think The Ex is 'the one' until you realize a few months or years down the road they were 'a' one. There are, of course, the stories of people who met in their 20s, were separated by the course of life and came back together 20 years later, and their love was unchanged. However, most people can and will have a relationship with someone else, even after losing the person they classed as their soul mate. That's not to say they didn't love both; it's just a different love with a different 'one' for them.

There is no right or wrong way to live your life with relationships. If you want to stay single to work on yourself, do it. If you want to date every day of the week, do it. Your person will come along, you will never know when.

There are no rules for how you meet someone. The main thing is that to meet someone, you just need to meet people and be out there somehow – whether it be speed dating, salsa, cycle club, football chat rooms or at work. You need to meet people.

Meeting people at the stage they're at

Am I ready for another relationship in the weeks following the breakup? No! Do I go on dates? Of course I do! I'm so thin from the stress of breaking up and the move I look blooming hot. Jeans and tops have never made me look so great. I have constantly been complimented on the weight loss and how good I look.

I am meeting guys to experience dating people other than The Ex, which is a necessary step in my view. Others wait until they are ready for the soul mate search. I, on the other hand, just felt I needed to talk to guys again and enjoy a conversation. It's almost like I had forgotten how to talk to people and what to talk about when I was on a date.

Some of the guys I dated were keen to see me again. However, my heartstrings were still connected to The Ex. Although I was on dates, I was comparing them to him and wishing I were with him. That may not have been fair on these guys (although I always went 50/50 on food and/or drinks), but I needed to date and I did hope to meet someone that would make me forget the Ex and move on. I was never rude to anyone, and I was always conscious of others' feelings. There's no reason to be mean to others, even if you know within a few minutes you don't have a connection.

One date spent most of the night talking about his Ex, who cheated on him. Going on our date must have been a cheap way to get counselling and get out there. Making The Ex the main topic of conversation is definitely not the way to move on. I needed to remind myself what I was looking for in a partner. Over time my heartstrings loosened, and finally, on one date, I really liked a guy and hoped to see him again.

You must accept that people out dating are at different phases of preparedness to meet someone. They also have to accept you at face value until they get to know you too. I didn't take being stood up, ghosted or not hearing from them again after a date personally. They didn't know me. They were dating at their stage of readiness, and I wouldn't know what that was. I wouldn't know the back history of this person, the drama or trauma they had experienced, so I couldn't take them not wanting to date me personally. They may have split up but got back together, they may have realized they weren't ready to date, or they may just not have felt a connection with me because they were still thinking of an Ex. So I couldn't be offended or take the lack of interest personally.

Dealing with dating setbacks

In the same vein of accepting people for where they are, it's worth remembering that dating people can hurt. I experienced some men who were quite inconsiderate of my time. I accepted that late arrivals or no shows were expected, but sometimes it can lead you to feel a bit low.

The other thing that has hurt me is when I feel like I have finally moved on. I have started dating someone I feel I like, and I feel they like me. I started to get excited about messaging them and hearing from them. We develop little insider jokes between us and little habits we do together. We both like a certain programme each week, or we sit at the same table at a local restaurant. Then it all goes wrong.

Then I didn't hear from them, or I heard back from them, but they are too busy to meet up any day soon or say they will get back to me later but don't. Clearly, something has switched off for them, and rationally I can't change that, but it hurts.

I will then say that I shouldn't have let my guard down with this guy. The relationship was too early to get too upset about. In other words, I shouldn't have started to get excited about this budding into a relationship. I should have protected myself. But why? Yes, it hurts, but I had no idea it would go this way. Why do I then beat myself up?

I've heard so many friends say the same, that they shouldn't have let their guard down. But how can we enjoy dating and feeling excited about someone without letting our guard down a little? Every time I started to get excited about a date, I would tell myself – or even friends would tell me – 'Don't get too invested; it can end any time, play it cool.'

I didn't come off as over keen or overly available. I didn't drop everything to see them but made the time I could in a reasonable timeframe. I would sometimes bend plans to see them but not too frequently that I lost my routine. But I would allow myself to get butterflies because liking someone is the best feeling. Feeling that someone has the potential to become something or someone special is wonderful.

It's not impossible, but it's very hard to meet someone when you're still mentally tied to The Ex. I had a friend that was tied to an Ex for five years. She hadn't spoken to them in over three years, but she was convinced that they would rekindle their relationship at some point. She had relationships that lasted a year or so, but each time, they failed because they were not The Ex. She missed their conversations, their habits. Everyone she tried to date wasn't The Ex. She tried to set up a routine like the one she had with The Ex, but these new boyfriends were not The Ex, so the routines were not the same.

I watched this happening, determined that I wouldn't hold such a place in my heart for someone like that. She overcame it when I finally convinced her to contact him and see if he responded. She could see that he had read the message, but he didn't reply. She was heartbroken. I honestly think she believed when they finally made contact, it would just start up again. That they were just waiting for this unspecified time when they were ready. The rejection of the no reply was like the relationship had ended all over again because the hope she held, even five years later, had finally ended. I think she needed to do that to finally move on. She very surprisingly met a guy on a night out with friends around six months later and within a year was engaged and moved in together, and several years later they are married and have a little one.

It was very hard for my friend to see a new person when she was holding on so strongly to the thought of The Ex. No two people are the same, and it's rare from my experience of friends who have done this that they have space in their heart for a new person when holding onto The Ex. My friend believed The Ex was 'The One' but she later realized he was just 'A One'.

When you are focusing so much on what you don't want and things that you haven't liked about your previous relationships, I feel it gets hard to think about what you do want. So I decided to manifest my partner into existence. I knew if I really wanted to meet someone, then I had to be clear about what it was I wanted. There was nothing materialistic on my list but it included aspects such as, 'I feel safe with them' and 'we are a team'.

I took the time to write this list down. I really considered what it was that I wanted. I carried it with me for a while after I decided it was complete. This was a useful exercise in focusing my mind on what I was looking for and reminding me I was single because The Ex hadn't met those standards.

Shortly before getting married, I found this list again when we were moving, and I can say my husband-to-be met everything on that list.

Meeting someone

One day, you will have that one date. You will go along, not expecting much but hoping you're on a fun date. Something about them is good and positive. You like what you're hearing. You like what they are wearing and how they move as they talk, their mannerisms.

You like yourself on the date, something in you shines. You talk, and the time flies. How did that date go so quickly? It's late. Better head off. They mention a second date, and you're glad they asked because you wanted to ask.

You text them, and they text you. You have butterflies, thinking it could all end any time. But it doesn't.

They share that they like you, and you like them.

You have a third date, a fourth date, then a few dates later, a weekend away. Time goes on, and then you go on holiday.

You both say you love the other.

A first row, a second row, you make it through. Then you move in together.

Birthdays and special events pass.

How were you ever so afraid that you wouldn't meet anyone?

In a nutshell

- When you start dating again, enjoy the warm fuzzy feeling of having a crush. Don't think too much about it. Just enjoy it.
- Having excited crush feelings for someone may not lead to a relationship, but that's how dating goes. Don't let that distract you from just enjoying meeting other people.
- There are so many ways to meet people. Do whatever you enjoy that brings you closer to others. Keep it light-hearted and fun.
- If going on dates, remember you don't need every single person you date to want to start a relationship after a few dates. You just need the right one. Don't be disheartened if, after meeting a few people, you haven't met someone you click with.
- Be kind to others and don't mess them around.
- You may meet some lovely people dating. You may also meet some obnoxious ones. Unfortunately, it's a bit of a lottery. Again, don't take anyone negative to heart as people are at different stages of their life and some may have had a difficult breakup and not have this handbook to help them.
- Trust that one day it will just happen. You won't know when or who. But one minute you're single, then the next you don't know how life was before they were in it.

Get out your notebook

- Write out qualities you would like in a new partner, things you hope they are interested in and things you could do together.
- How do you want to feel in your next relationship? The more you project forward what you want, the more likely you will spot it when you find it.

If you don't have your happy ending, it's just because your story isn't over yet.

Conclusion

You Never Know How Your Story Will Turn Out

Time will tell how your life will go and whether you find the right partner, get the career you wanted, live in the house you always dreamed of and have a life full of great times. What is clear is that being in the wrong relationship can hold you back from your dreams, make you depressed, cause you to miss out on great times and ultimately make you feel pretty awful about yourself. It is better, in my view, to be single, investing the precious time I have into wider experiences that life has to offer, finding ways to do things for myself and making the most of my free time. When I split up from someone, it felt like the end of the world, but each time it happened, I propelled myself into many great life experiences, events and fun times.

I'd rather spend my time alone with the potential to find love than waste time with someone not right for me

---

Over time I've seen my friends' relationships that I thought would last fail. I've been part of the bridal shower for friends who used to think they would never meet anyone. I've seen friends bring babies into this world. I have seen the patterns of the breakups and makeups, the people who treated partners badly from one to the next. I've seen relationships I thought would fail, evolve and survive the test of time as couples have put the time in to make it work, fought to stay together and built things together. I've seen a friend with potential be dragged down by the wrong person and helped them after the breakup to remind them of who they are.

I love a movie montage, and now I am older, I know how all the stories of the relationships of my youth play out. I wish I had this book when I was so heartbroken that I couldn't get out of bed. Those first heartbreaks when I thought there was no one else out there for me until there was, and I fell in love again, and that relationship also failed. The amazing trips I planned when the relationships ended and the experiences I'd denied myself to appease being in a bad relationship at the time.

Keep faith if you feel that your relationship ended and you didn't expect it to; if you allow yourself to feel good about this and use this as an opportunity, this breakup will be the best thing that happened to you. The breakup can help you move on from the wrong person and teach you what you need to find the right one.

So just because this hurts now doesn't mean you will feel this way forever, or even for longer than a few weeks. In time, you will look at these breakups and be glad that you became available to live life to the full again.

I guess what I realized is that my story, the story that is me, has many plot turns and chapters left in it yet. I can still be anyone. My story, my life is not over yet. It's my decision whether this story has a happy ending.

About the Author

Liann Brookes-Smith lives in Birmingham with her husband and two sons. An avid reader of self-help books and modern psychology, she is always keen to understand the why underlining her thoughts and actions.

She has travelled the world, living in Africa, Australia and South America and experienced dating woes on at least three continents.

This is the first book in *The Handbook* series.

Printed in Great Britain
by Amazon

79797990R00122